CREATING SOUNDS
Or: How to Use All Those Buttons and Switches

CONTENTS

AVAILABLE VOICES 4
THINK OF THE SONG 5
VOICE CHARACTERISTICS 8
USING THE EFFECTS 9
CHOOSING A VOICE TO FIT THE MOOD 10
DON'T FORGET THE RHYTHM 11

SONG EXCERPTS: See Page 48 for listing.

CLARINET 12
FLUTE 14
OBOE 16
SAXOPHONE 18
TRUMPET 20
TROMBONE 22
STRINGS/VIOLIN 24
CELLO 26
VIBES 27
PIANO/ELECTRIC PIANO 28
HARPSICHORD 30
ACCORDION 31
GUITAR 32
ELECTRIC GUITAR 33
STEEL GUITAR/HAWAIIAN GUITAR 34
CLASSICAL GUITAR 35
BANJO 36
MANDOLIN 37
ORGAN/CHURCH ORGAN/PIPE ORGAN 38
CELESTE/CHIMES 41
HORN/FRENCH HORN 42
SYNTHESIZED VOICES 44
THE HOW TO'S OF EASY ABC MUSIC FOR BEGINNERS 46

Copyright © 1994 by HAL LEONARD CORPORATION
International Copyright Secured   All Rights Reserved

For all works contained herein:
Unauthorized copying, arranging, adapting, recording or
  public performance is an infringement of copyright.
Infringers are liable under the law.

E-Z PLAY ® TODAY Music Notation © 1975 HAL LEONARD CORPORATION
E-Z PLAY and EASY ELECTRONIC KEYBOARD MUSIC are
  registered trademarks of HAL LEONARD CORPORATION

A JOINT PUBLICATION OF

EXCLUSIVELY DISTRIBUTED BY

7777 W. BLUEMOUND RD. P.O. BOX 13819 MILWAUKEE, WI 53213

AVAILABLE VOICES _____

THINK OF THE SONG

Try this with a song most people will recognize. Think of the song SKATER'S WALTZ. Close your eyes and imagine the melody. Hum it to yourself. **Feel** the song. **See** the music.

Now, think of the mood and feeling. The length of the notes can add to a feeling. Are the notes long and flowing, or short and bouncing? Picture the setting of this song. What does the song make you think of?

Play SKATER'S WALTZ, using the elements you just imagined. The suggestions and song characteristics before the song will be found throughout the book. They are listed to help you better match the voices and rhythms to the kind of song you want to play.

THE SKATERS

Voice: ORGAN
Rhythm: Slow WALTZ

Mood: Smooth, flowing

By EMIL WALDTEUFEL

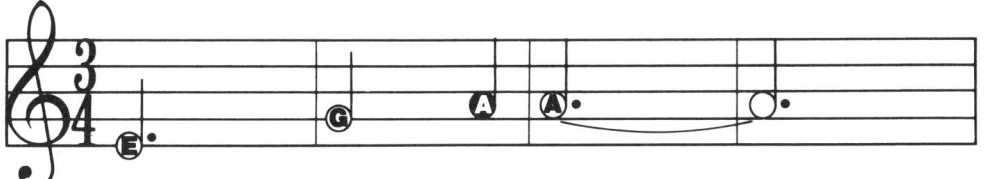

Copyright © 1994 by HAL LEONARD CORPORATION
International Copyright Secured   All Rights Reserved

VOICE CHARACTERISTICS

*ALL SONGS HAVE A STYLE & MOOD. THE VOICES YOU USE HAVE MOODS & STYLES, TOO. THE FOLLOWING ILLUSTRATIONS SHOW GROUPINGS OF VOICES ACCORDING TO THEIR **TONE SUSPENSION** (HOW LONG A NOTE SOUNDS AFTER PRESSING THE KEY) & **ATTACK SPEED**) (HOW QUICKLY A NOTE SOUNDS AFTER PRESSING THE KEY).*

CONTINUOUS TONE - Sounds as long as you hold down a key.

Instruments with continuous tones include: organ, horns, accordion, trumpet, trombone, strings, oboe, flute, saxophone and clarinet.

DECAY - Tone fades away.

Piano, harpsichord, banjo, guitar, harp, chimes, celeste, vibes, marimba, xylophone.

PERCUSSIVE - Strong, accented attack.

Instruments that are plucked or struck, such as piano, banjo, etc. Same as Decay group.

SLOW ATTACK - Powered by air, causing delay in tone.

Accordion, bagpipe, calliope, harmonica, pipe organ.

Notice that certain voices can be found in more than one group. For instance, the organ voice has a slow attack quality but it sounds as long as you hold down the key. It has a continuous tone with slow attack.

> YOUR KEYBOARD'S **EFFECTS** ADD COLOR & REALISM TO MANY OF THE INSTRUMENTAL SOUNDS YOU'll USE. FOR EXAMPLE, USE YOUR ORGAN VOICE WITH VIBRATO OR TREMOLO & IT SOUNDS LIKE A THEATER ORGAN. USE IT WITH REVERB AND IT'S A CHURCH ORGAN!

Name	Characteristic	What it does for you	Where to use it
Vibrato	Rapid changes in pitch	Adds warmth and expression to your playing.	Violin family, most woodwind, reed, and brass instruments.
Sustain	Tone fades slowly away after key is released.	"Fills in" around the notes you play . . . smooth sound.	Slower songs. Good for chime and other bell-like effects.
Tremolo	Rapid changes in volume.	Adds life to your music with a pulsating effect.	Popular and theater songs, fast or slow . . . "full organ" effects. Mainly flute-type voices.
Chorale (Slow Tremolo)	Slow changes in volume	Your music seems to swirl around the room . . . an exciting effect.	Mostly with flute-type voices . . . jazz and rock tunes. Also religious songs. Try it with strings and chorus combined.
Reverb	Echo-like quality.	Sounds like you're in a concert hall or an arena. Puts "presence" in your playing.	Use a little on most music. Full reverb can create a "spacey" effect for some songs.
Chorus	Sounds like more than one voice	Adds a spacious dimension to the notes you play.	Almost anywhere. Create a string ensemble or a brass section. Try it with Chorale or Tremolo.
Percussion	Strong initial attack on each tone.	Creates effects of instruments that are plucked (guitar) or struck (piano).	Imitating various instruments. Also for various jazz and rock organ effects.
Portamento	Slide effect from note to note.	Creates eerie mysterious or "outerspace" feeling.	Use for modern tunes with space theme - great with synthe voices
Stereo		Multi-speaker "3-D" sound.	Use for strong loud or expressive songs.

Below are definitions of general sounds found for each song in the books listed on page 48. These instructions are to help you better associate certain voices on your keyboard with the sound and feel of a particular song. Below these, a chart matches instrument voices to the General Sound of a song.

FULL 'N' BRILLIANT - Big, full theater organ sounds for show tunes or standards from the big band era.
FULL 'N' MELLOW - Flute and horn sounds ideal for ballads or waltzes.
BRIGHT 'N' BRASSY - Sounds best suited for swing tunes, rock, polkas or marches.
BIG 'N' BOLD - Jazz and rock tunes sound their best when you use this category.
SOFT SOLO - Beautiful solo voices like the piano, vibes or clarinet create a quiet mood.
BRILLIANT SOLO - Brighter voices like the trumpet, oboe, saxophone, banjo and mandolin for playing dixieland, swing, polkas or rock tunes.
CLASSICAL - For playing classical or religious music as well as your favorite Christmas carols.

SOFT SOLO	BRILLIANT SOLO	FULL 'N' BRILLIANT	FULL 'N' MELLOW	BRIGHT 'N' BRASSY	BIG 'N' BOLD	CLASSICAL
	Accordion	Accordion		Accordion		
	Banjo/Mandolin					
	Brass/Brass Ensemble	Brass/Brass Ensemble		Brass/Brass Ensemble	Brass/Brass Ensemble	Brass/Brass Ensemble
Cello			Cello			Cello
		Chimes				
Clarinet	Clarinet	Clarinet	Clarinet	Clarinet		
Flute			Flute			
Guitar	Guitar/Elec. Guitar		Guitar/Elec. Guitar		Guitar/Elec. Guitar	Guitar/Classical Guitar
Harpsichord						Harpsichord
Horn	Horn	Horn	Horn	Horn	Horn	Horn
Marimba						
Oboe	Oboe					Oboe
		Organ	Organ			Organ
Piano/Elec. Piano	Piano/Elec. Piano	Piano	Piano	Piano	Piano/Elec. Piano	Piano
Reed	Reed					Reed
	Saxophone	Saxophone		Saxophone	Saxophone	
Strings/Violin	Strings/Violin	Strings/Violin	Strings/Violin			Strings/Violin
						String/Ensemble
Trombone		Trombone	Trombone	Trombone	Trombone	
	Trumpet	Trumpet		Trumpet	Trumpet	
Vibes						
	Xylophone					

Just as you hear an instrument sound when you think of a song, you must also think of the rhythm, or beat.

Is it a Waltz? A Rhumba?

This chart shows you the general mood a rhythm creates and some good voices to use with them.

Rhythm or style	General mood	Possible voices
Bossa nova	soft, floating, sensuous	flute, piano, guitar
Rock/Disco	hard-driving, very rhythmic	guitar, organ, brass, synthesizer
Rhumba/Beguine	varies depending on song	marimba, brass, vibes
March	martial, brassy and percussive	brass, trumpet, sax
Polka	happy, loud, danceable	accordion, clarinet, brass
Swing	jazz flavor or "big bands"	brass family, vibes, sax
Waltz	soft, romantic	strings, piano, mandolin
Ballad/Slow Rock	expressive, romantic	flute, piano, string, clarinet

You are now ready to apply what you've learned. The following songs appear in groups according to which instrument voice would sound good for the song. Two or three songs using the clarinet voice will appear together, etc. Each song is accompanied by suggestions for voice selection, mood, and rhythm. Remember, these are only suggestions. Experiment with any element or combination of elements until the song sounds best to you!

CLARINET
Optional Substitutes:
FLUTE, STRINGS/VIOLIN

TAKE MY BREATH AWAY
(LOVE THEME)

CLARINET
SOFT SOLO
Medium Slow ROCK

Words and Music by GIORGIO MORODER
and TOM WHITLOCK

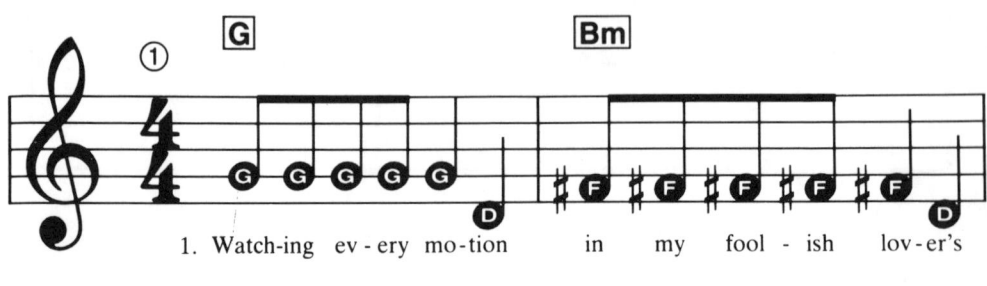

1. Watch-ing ev-ery mo-tion in my fool-ish lov-er's

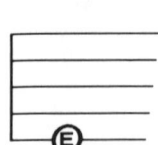

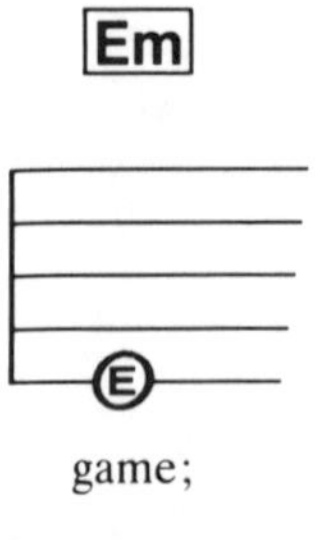

game;

Copyright © 1986 by Famous Music Corporation and Budde Music, Inc.
All Rights on behalf of Budde Music, Inc. Administered by WB Music Corp.
International Copyright Secured   All Rights Reserved

TOO FAT POLKA
(SHE'S TOO FAT FOR ME)

CLARINET
BRIGHT 'N' BRASSY
Medium Fast POLKA

Words and Music by ROSS MacLEAN
and ARTHUR RICHARDSON

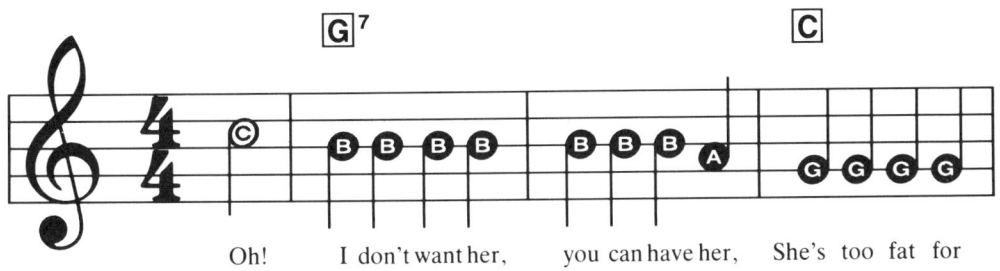

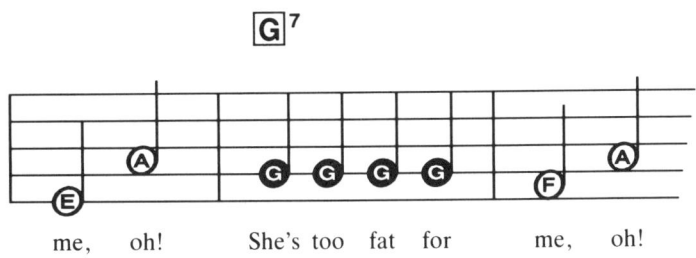

Copyright © 1947 Shapiro, Bernstein & Co., Inc., New York
Copyright Renewed
International Copyright Secured   All Rights Reserved

SAILING

CLARINET
FULL 'N' MELLOW
Medium BALLAD

Words and Music by
CHRISTOPHER CROSS

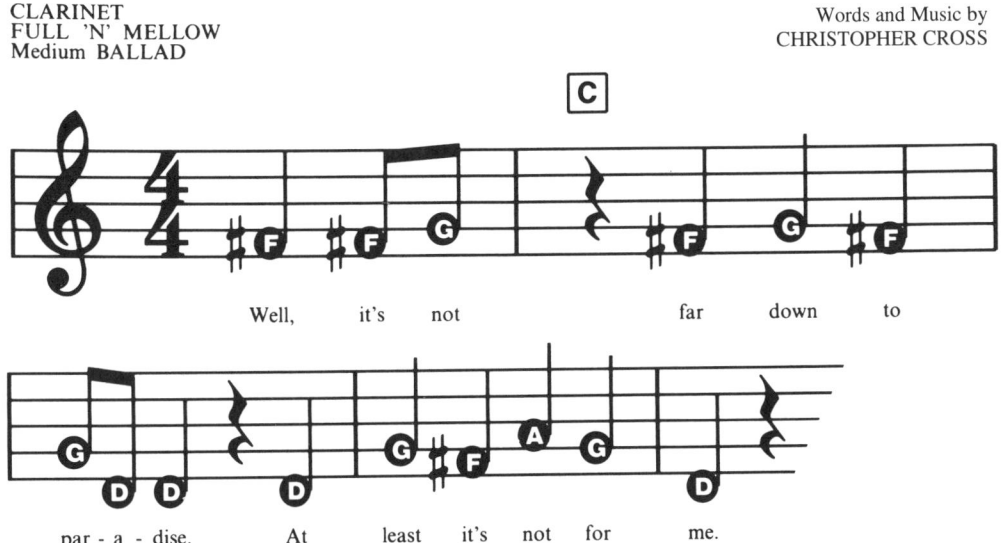

Copyright © 1979 BMG Songs, Inc.
International Copyright Secured   All Rights Reserved

FLUTE
Optional Substitutes:
CLARINET, STRINGS/VIOLIN

I JUST CALLED TO SAY I LOVE YOU

FLUTE
FULL 'N' MELLOW
Medium ROCK

Words and Music by
STEVIE WONDER

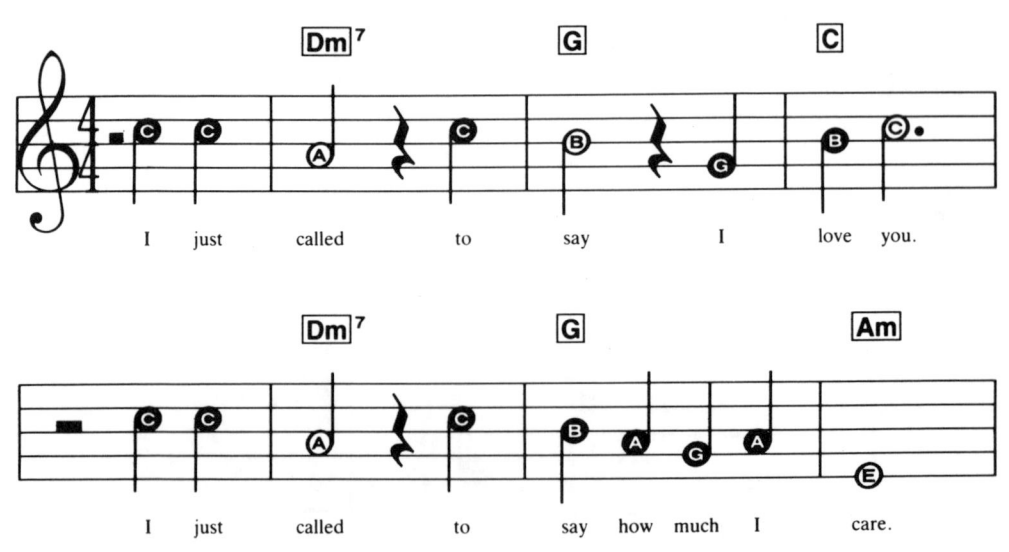

Copyright © 1984 by JOBETE MUSIC CO., INC. and BLACK BULL MUSIC, INC.
International Copyright Secured   All Rights Reserved

A TIME FOR US
(LOVE THEME)

Words by LARRY KUSIK
and EDDIE SNYDER
Music by NINO ROTA

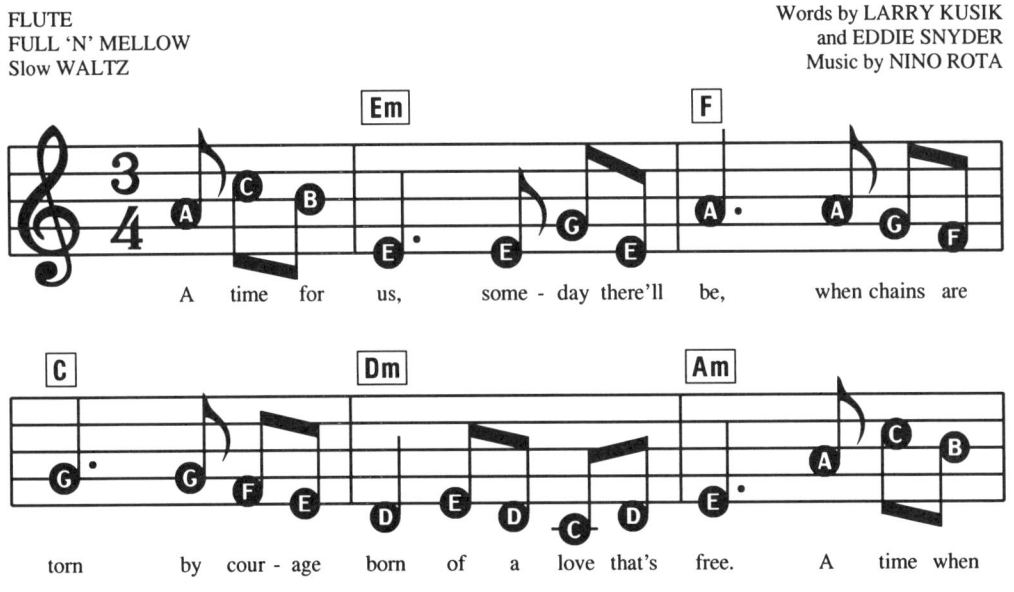

Copyright © 1968 by Famous Music Corporation
International Copyright Secured   All Rights Reserved

WHAT'S LOVE GOT TO DO WITH IT

Words and Music by TERRY BRITTEN
and GRAHAM LYLE

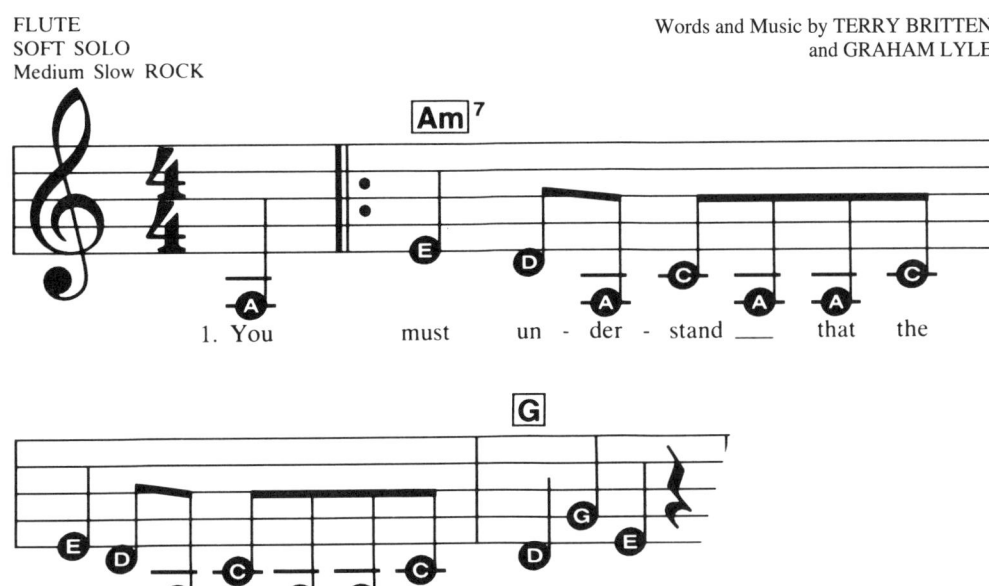

Copyright © 1984 by Myaxe Music Ltd. and Good Single Music Ltd.
This arrangement Copyright © 1994 by Myaxe Music Ltd. and Good Single Music Ltd.
All Rights for Myaxe Music Ltd. Administered in the U.S.A. by Chappell & Co.
International Copyright Secured   All Rights Reserved

OBOE
Optional Substitutes:
CLARINET, FLUTE, STRINGS/VIOLIN

RHIANNON

Words and Music by
STEVIE NICKS

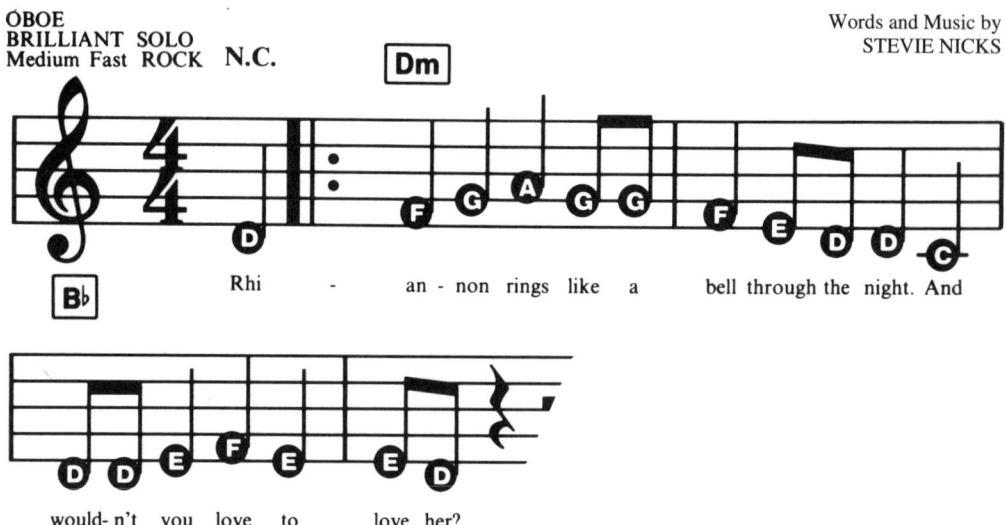

Copyright © 1975 Welsh Witch Music
All Rights Administered by Sony Music Publishing, 8 Music Square West, Nashville, TN 37203
International Copyright Secured   All Rights Reserved

OBOE
BRILLIANT SOLO
Slow WALTZ

COVENTRY CAROL

TRADITIONAL BRITISH

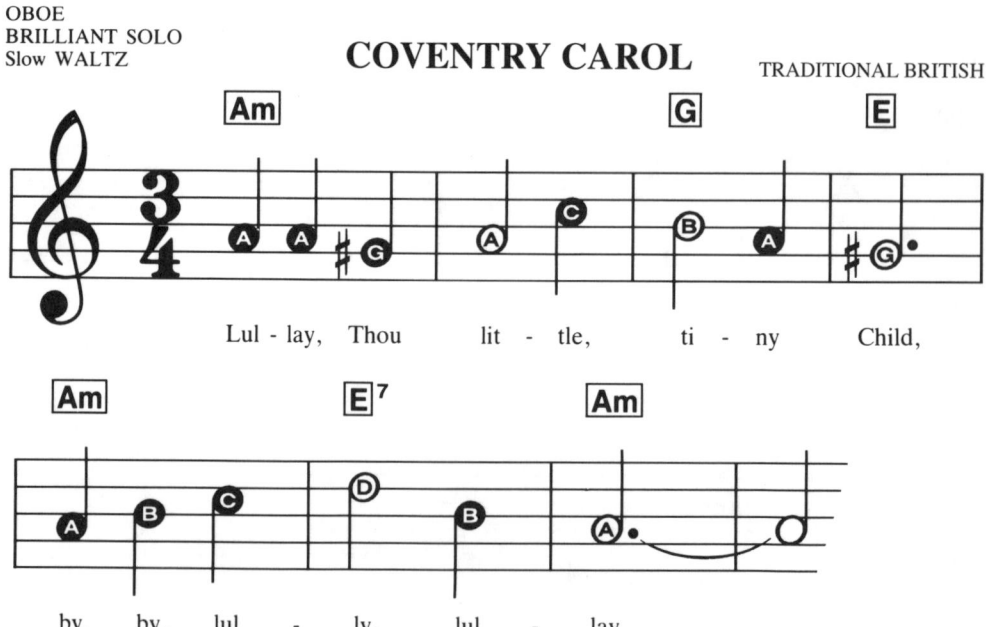

16
Copyright © 1994 by HAL LEONARD CORPORATION
International Copyright Secured   All Rights Reserved

CARAVAN

OBOE
FULL 'N' MELLOW
Fast BALLAD

Words and Music by DUKE ELLINGTON,
IRVING MILLS and JUAN TIZOL

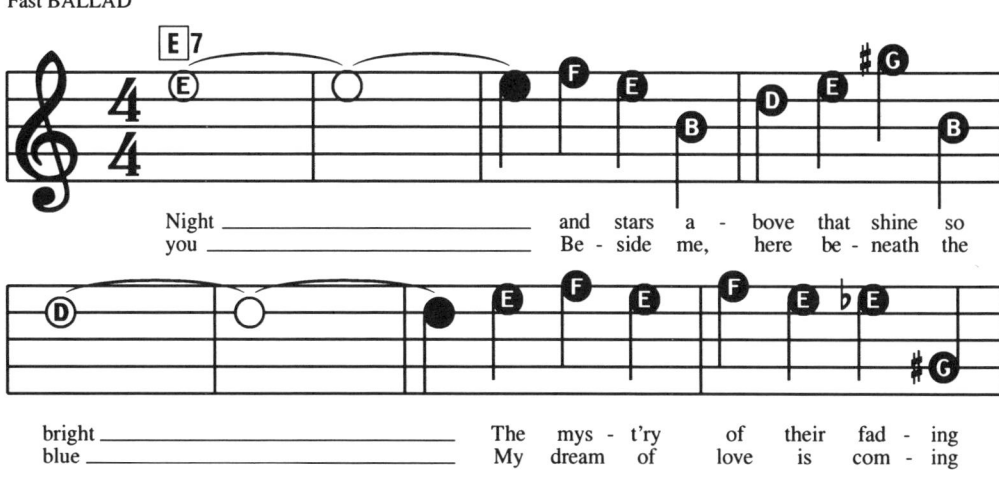

Copyright © 1937 (Renewed 1965) and Assigned to Famous Music Corporation and EMI Mills Music Inc. in the U.S.A.
Rights for the world outside the U.S.A. Controlled by EMI Mills Music Inc. and CPP/Belwin, Inc.
International Copyright Secured   All Rights Reserved

GOING HOME
(Symphony No. 5, "From The New World")

OBOE
CLASSICAL
No Rhythm

By ANTONIN DVORAK

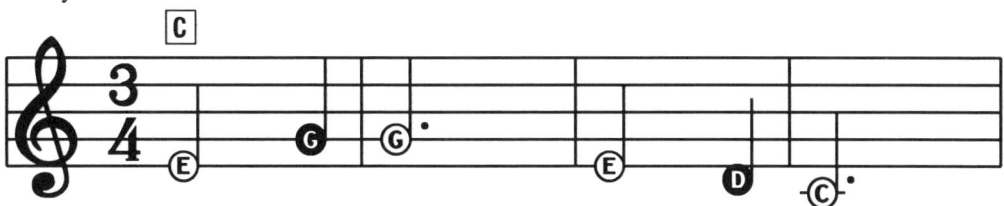

Copyright © 1994 by HAL LEONARD CORPORATION
International Copyright Secured   All Rights Reserved

17

SAXOPHONE
Optional Substitutes:
FLUTE, TRUMPET, TROMBONE

SAXOPHONE
BRILLIANT SOLO
Med. Fast SWING

IN THE MOOD

Words and Music by
JOE GARLAND

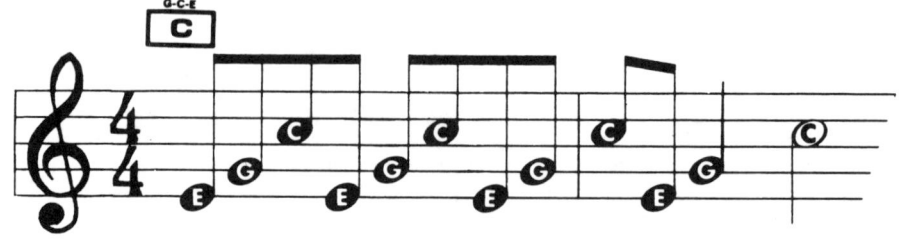

Copyright © 1939, 1960 Shapiro, Bernstein & Co., Inc., New York
Copyright Renewed
International Copyright Secured   All Rights Reserved   Used By Permission

JUST THE WAY YOU ARE

SAXOPHONE
FULL 'N' MELLOW
Medium ROCK

Words and Music by
BILLY JOEL

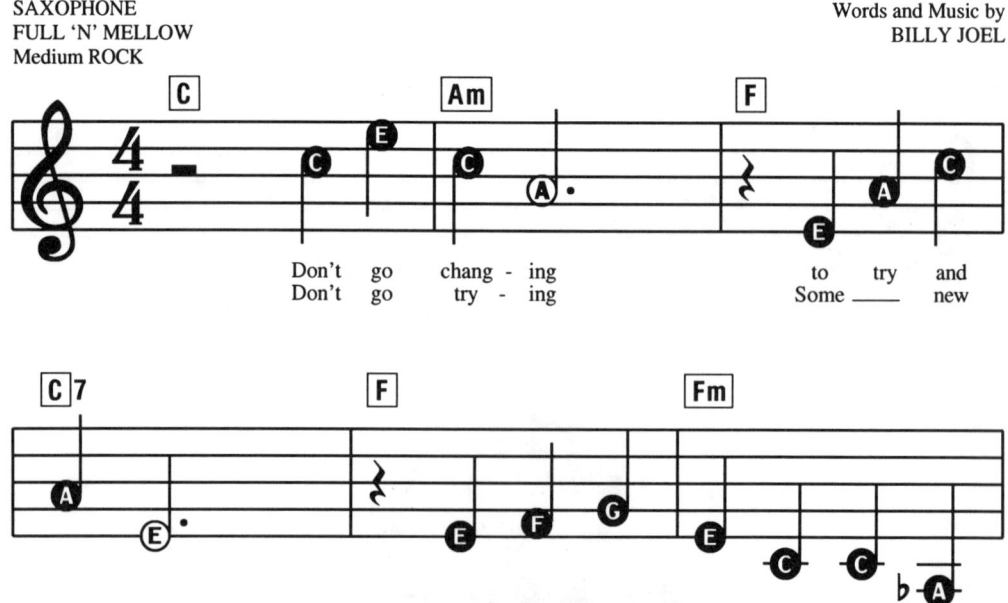

© 1977, 1978 IMPULSIVE MUSIC
This arrangement © 1994 IMPULSIVE MUSIC
All Rights Controlled and Administered by EMI APRIL MUSIC INC.
All Rights Reserved   International Copyright Secured   Used by Permission

THEME FROM NEW YORK, NEW YORK

SAXOPHONE
BIG 'N' BOLD
Medium SWING

Music by JOHN KANDER
Words by FRED EBB

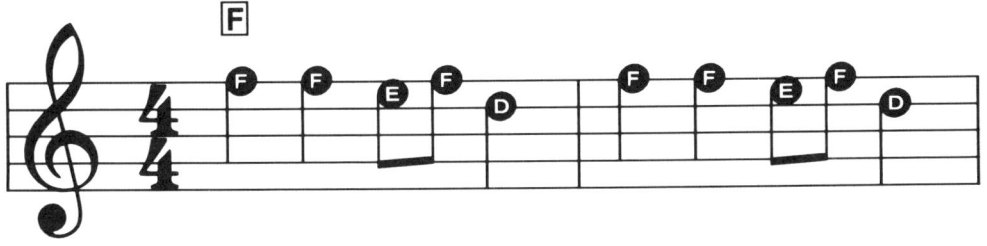

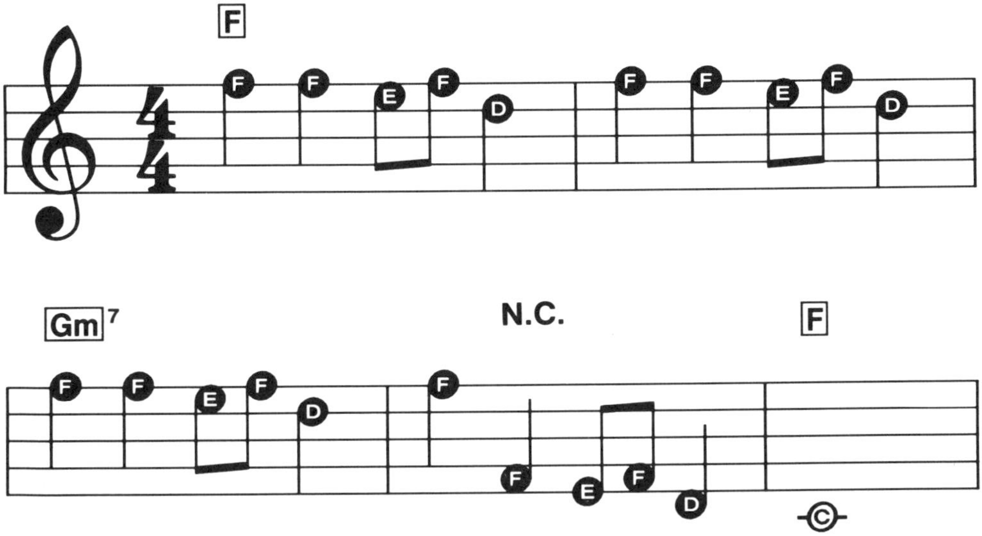

© 1977 UNITED ARTISTS CORPORATION
All Rights Controlled and Administered by EMI UNART CATALOG INC.
International Copyright Secured   All Rights Reserved

STAR DUST

SAXOPHONE
BRILLIANT SOLO
Medium SWING

Words by MITCHELL PARISH
Music by HOAGY CARMICHAEL

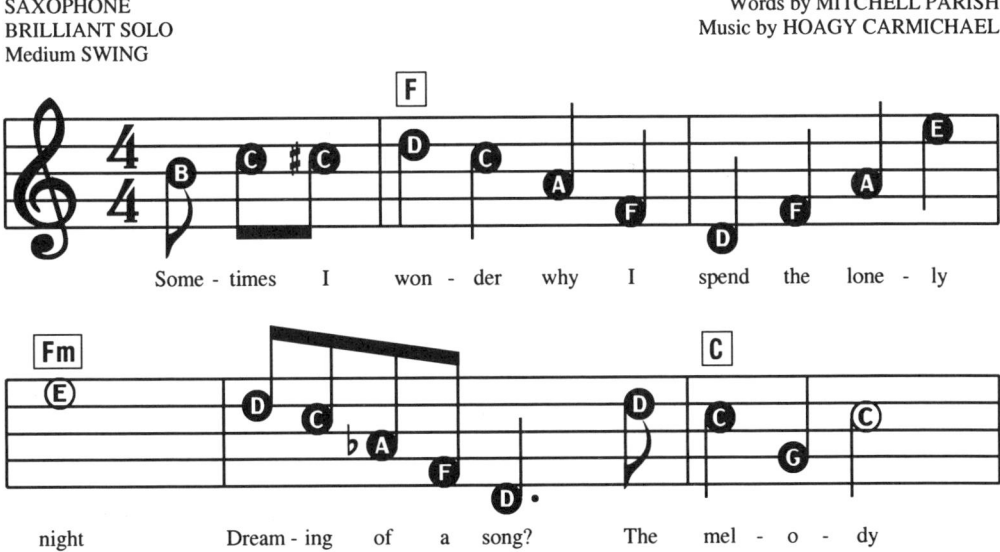

Copyright © 1929 (Renewed 1957) by Mills Music, Inc.
International Copyright Secured   All Rights Reserved

TRUMPET
Optional Subtitutes:
TROMBONE, SAXOPHONE

USE THE TROMBONE VOICE FOR THE LOW TO MIDDLE KEYBOARD RANGE SONGS AND THE SAXOPHONE OR CLARINET FOR THE HIGH KEYBOARD RANGE SONGS.

FIVE FOOT TWO, EYES OF BLUE
(HAS ANYBODY SEEN MY GIRL?)

TRUMPET
BIG 'N' BOLD
Medium Fast SWING

Words by JOE YOUNG and SAM LEWIS
Music by RAY HENDERSON

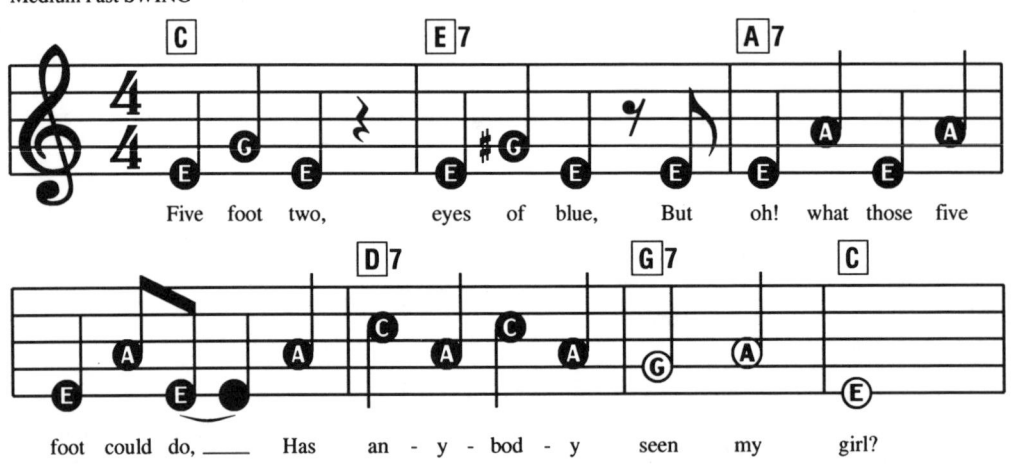

© 1925 LEO FEIST, INC.
© Renewed 1953 WAROCK CORP., LEO FEIST, INC. and HENDERSON MUSIC CO.
All Rights Reserved

AIN'T MISBEHAVIN'

TRUMPET
FULL 'N' BRILLIANT
Medium SWING

Words by ANDY RAZAF
Music by THOMAS WALLER and HARRY BROOKS

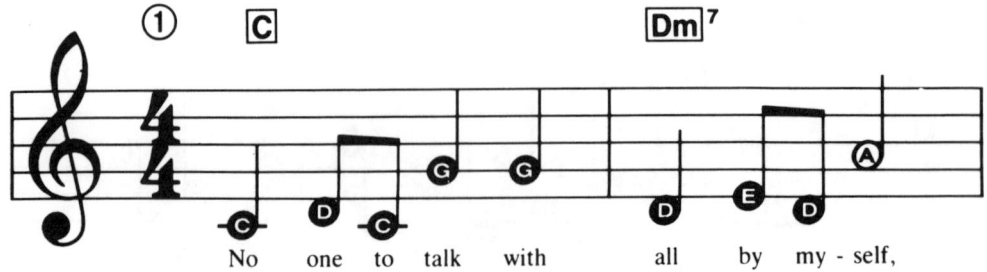

Copyright © 1929 by Mills Music, Inc.
Copyright Renewed, Waller's interest controlled by Chappell & Co.; Razaf's interest administered by The Songwriters Guild of America
International Copyright Secured   All Rights Reserved

INTO THE GROOVE

TRUMPET
BRIGHT 'N' BRASSY
Medium ROCK or DISCO

Words and Music by STEPHEN BRAY
and MADONNA CICCONE

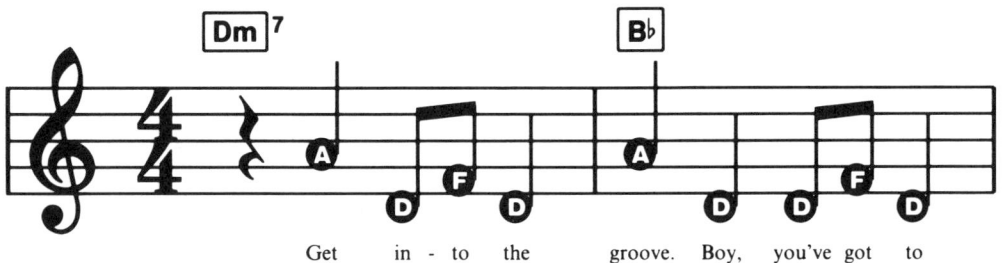

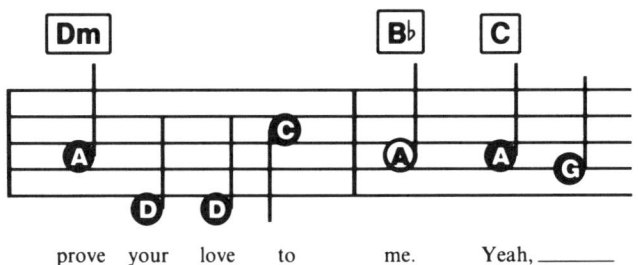

Copyright © 1985 Black Lion Music, WB Music Corp., Bleu Disque Music Co., Inc. and Webo Girl Publishing, Inc.
All rights on behalf of Bleu Disque Music Co., Inc. and Webo Girl Publishing, Inc. administered by WB Music Corp.
International Copyright Secured   All Rights Reserved

SIR DUKE

TRUMPET
BRILLIANT SOLO
Medium Slow ROCK

Words and Music by
STEVIE WONDER

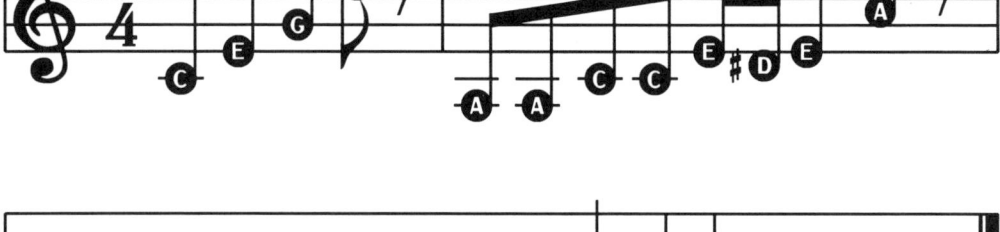

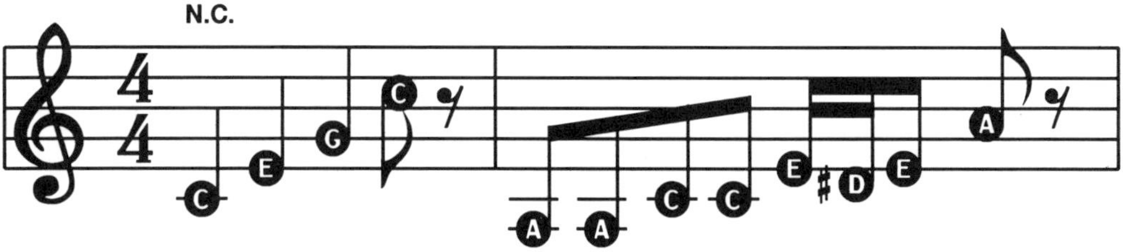

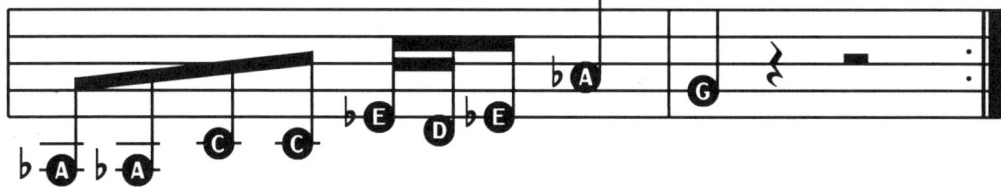

Copyright © 1976 by JOBETE MUSIC CO., INC. and BLACK BULL MUSIC, INC.
International Copyright Secured   All Rights Reserved

TROMBONE
Optional Substitutes:
CELLO, HORN, ORGAN, SAXOPHONE

STAND BY ME

TROMBONE
FULL 'N' MELLOW
Slow SWING

Words and Music by BEN E. KING,
JERRY LEIBER and MIKE STOLLER

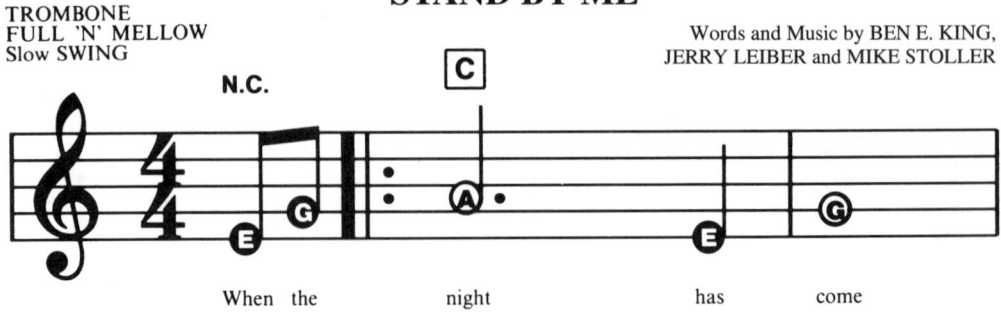

When the night has come

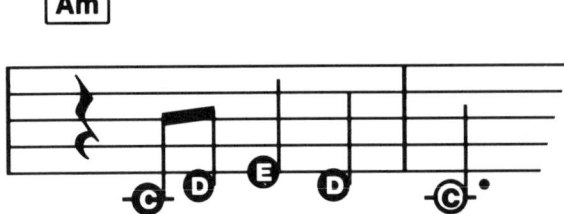

and the land is dark

Copyright © 1961 by Progressive Music Publishing Co., Trio Music, Inc. and ADT Enterprises Inc.
Copyright Renewed
All Rights for the U.S.A. and Canada Controlled by Intersong U.S.A., Inc. and Warner Bros. Music
International Copyright Secured   All Rights Reserved

I'M GETTING SENTIMENTAL OVER YOU

TROMBONE
FULL 'N' MELLOW
Medium SWING

Words by NED WASHINGTON
Music by GEORGE BASSMAN

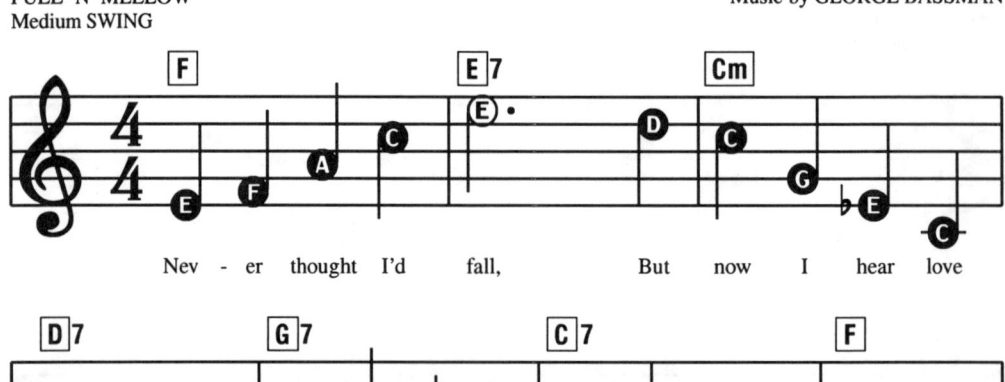

Nev - er thought I'd fall, But now I hear love

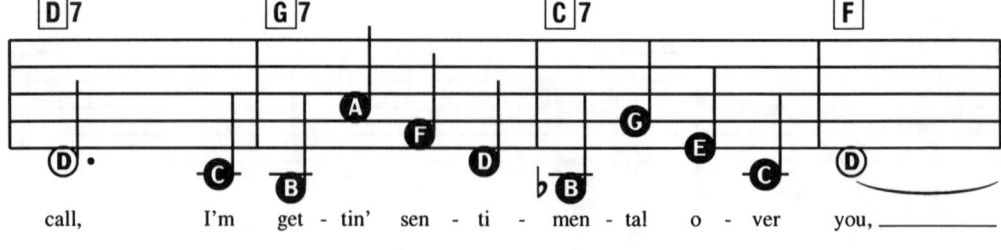

call, I'm get - tin' sen - ti - men - tal o - ver you,

Copyright © 1932 (Renewed) by Mills Music, Inc.
International Copyright Secured   All Rights Reserved

GEORGIA ON MY MIND

TROMBONE
BRIGHT 'N' BRASSY
Medium SWING

Words by STUART GORRELL
Music by HOAGY CARMICHAEL

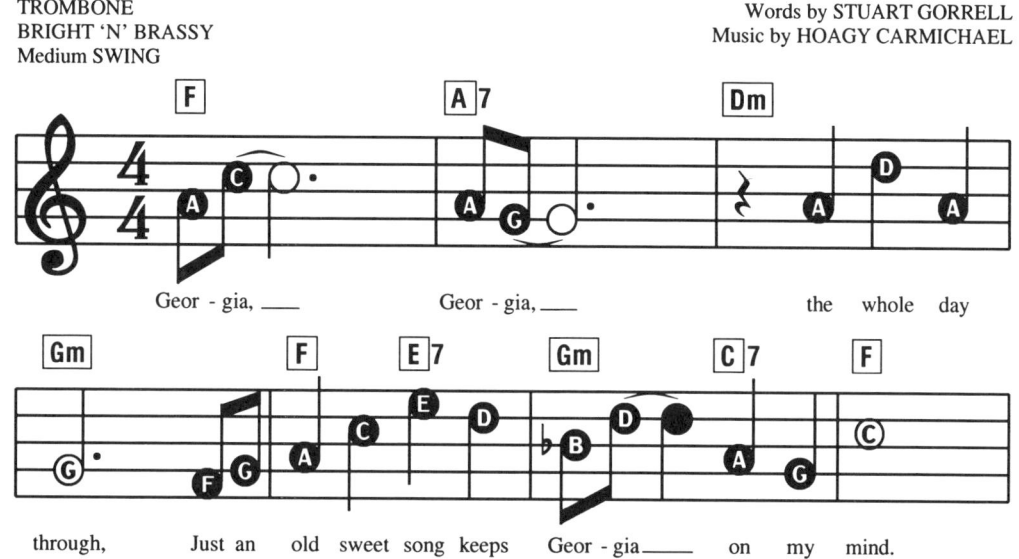

Copyright © 1930 by Peer Music Ltd.
Copyright Renewed
International Copyright Secured   All Rights Reserved

SUDDENLY

TROMBONE
FULL 'N' MELLOW
Medium Slow ROCK

Words and Music by KEITH DIAMOND
and BILLY OCEAN

© 1984 Willesden Music Inc./Keith Diamond Music/Zomba Music Publishers Ltd./Aqua Music Ltd.
All Rights for Keith Diamond Music controlled by Willesden Music Inc. for the world.
All Rights for Zomba Music Publishers Ltd. and Aqua Music Ltd. controlled by Zomba Enterprises Inc. for the U.S.A. & Canada.
International Copyright Secured   All Rights Reserved

23

STRINGS/VIOLIN
Optional Substitutes:
CLARINET, SAXOPHONE, PIANO, HORN, FLUTE

THEME FROM ICE CASTLES
(THROUGH THE EYES OF LOVE)

STRINGS
FULL 'N' MELLOW
Slow ROCK or BALLAD

Words by CAROLE BAYER SAGER
Music by MARVIN HAMLISCH

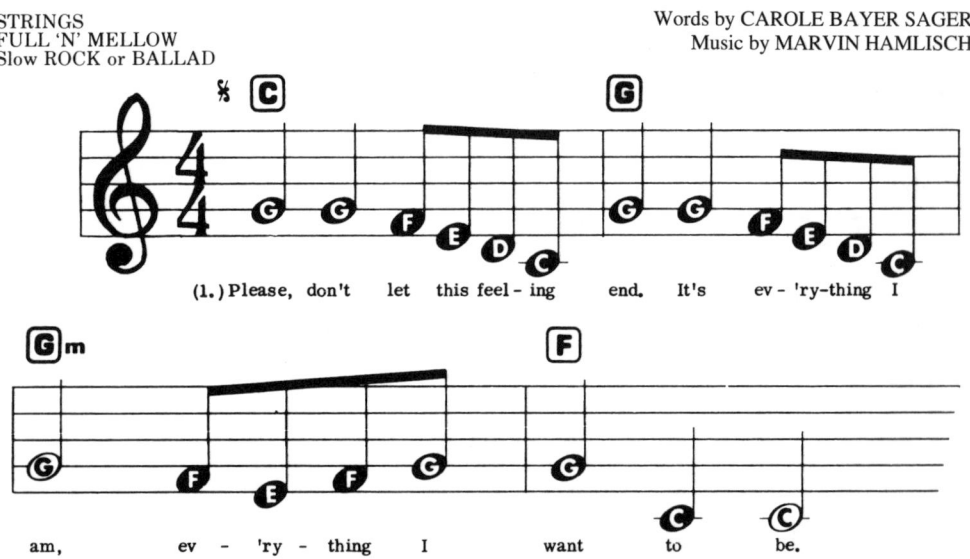

Copyright © 1978 by Gold Horizon Music Corp. and Golden Torch Music Corp.
International Copyright Secured   All Rights Reserved

CZARDAS

STRINGS
CLASSICAL
No Rhythm

BY VITTORIO MONTI

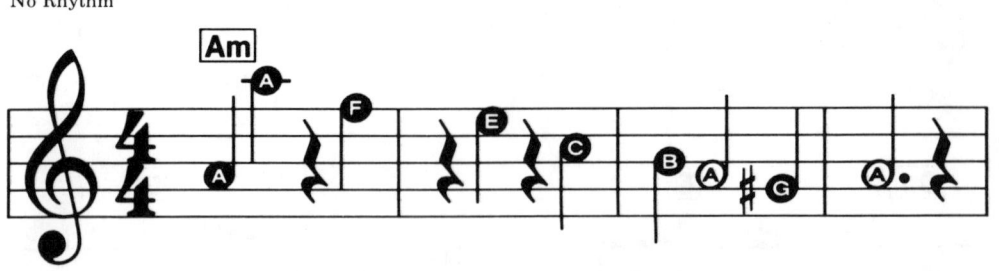

Copyright © 1994 by HAL LEONARD CORPORATION
International Copyright Secured   All Rights Reserved

MIDNIGHT COWBOY

VIOLIN
FULL 'N' BRILLIANT
Slow SHUFFLE

By JOHN BARRY

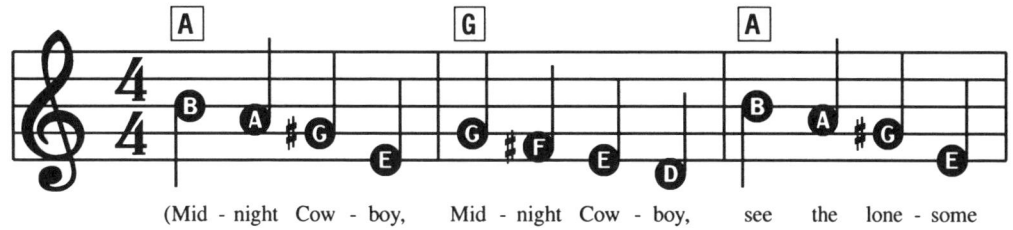

© 1969 by UNITED ARTISTS MUSIC CO., INC.
International Copyright Secured   All Rights Reserved

CRYING

VIOLIN
FULL 'N' MELLOW
Medium Slow SWING

Words and Music by ROY ORBISON
and JOE MELSON

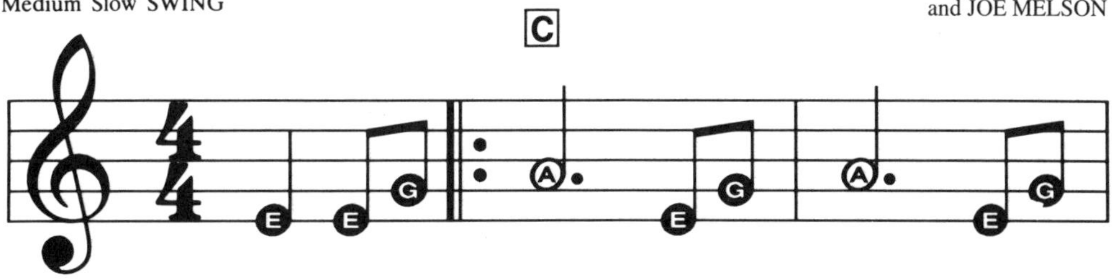

Copyright © 1961 (Renewed 1989) ORBI-LEE MUSIC, R-KEY DARKUS MUSIC and ACUFF-ROSE MUSIC, INC.
All rights on behalf of ORBI-LEE MUSIC and R-KEY DARKUS MUSIC administered by WARNER-TAMERLANE PUBLISHING CORP.
All Rights Reserved

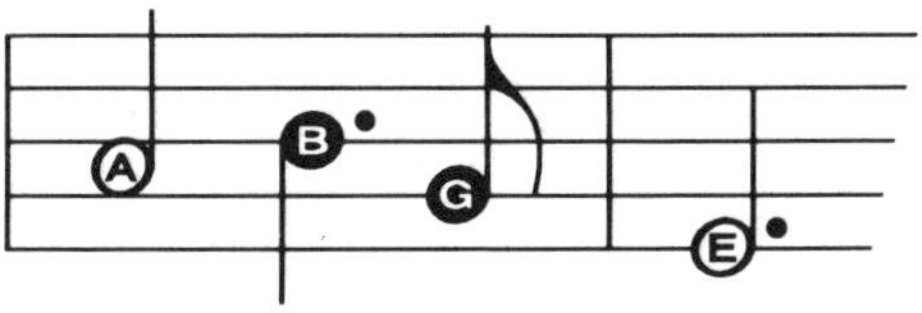

CELLO
Optional Substitutes:
STRINGS/VIOLIN, TROMBONE, ORGAN

TRUE COLORS

CELLO
SOFT SOLO
Slow ROCK

Words and Music by BILLY STEINBERG
and TOM KELLY

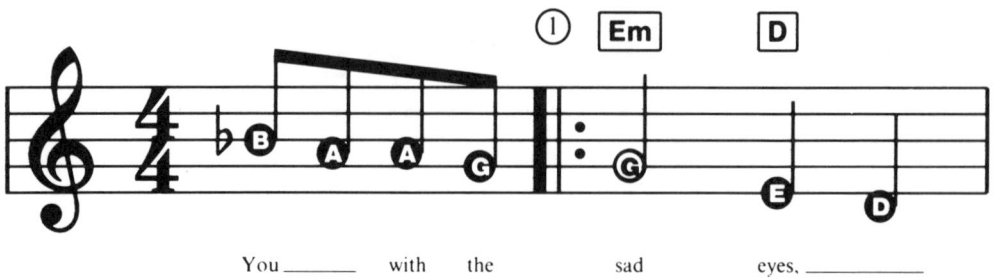

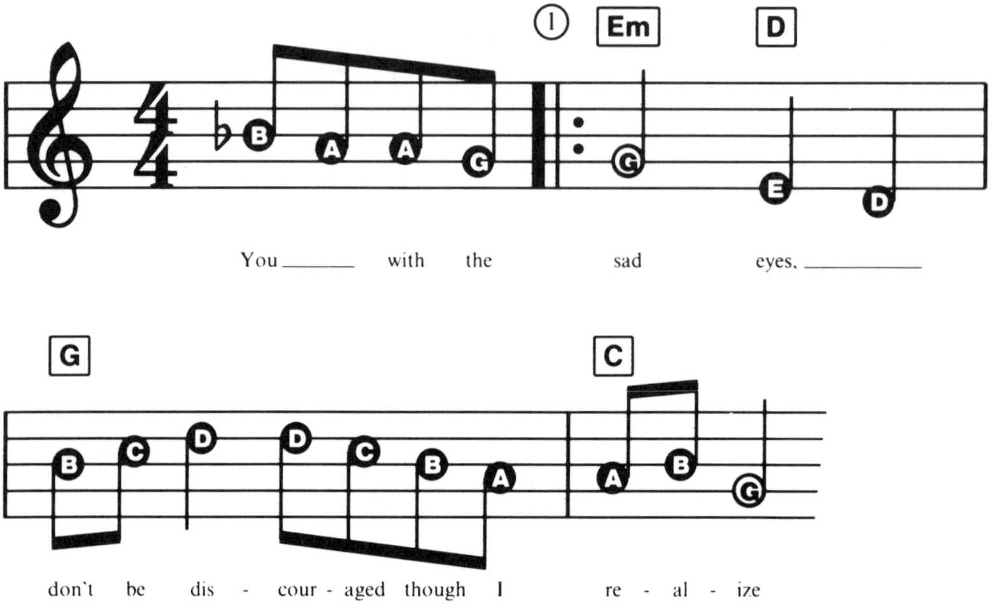

Copyright © 1986 Sony Tunes Inc.
All Rights Administered by Sony Music Publishing, 8 Music Square West, Nashville, TN 37203
International Copyright Secured   All Rights Reserved

SPEAK SOFTLY, LOVE
(LOVE THEME)

CELLO
SOFT SOLO
Medium Slow BALLAD

Words by LARRY KUSIK
Music by NINO ROTA

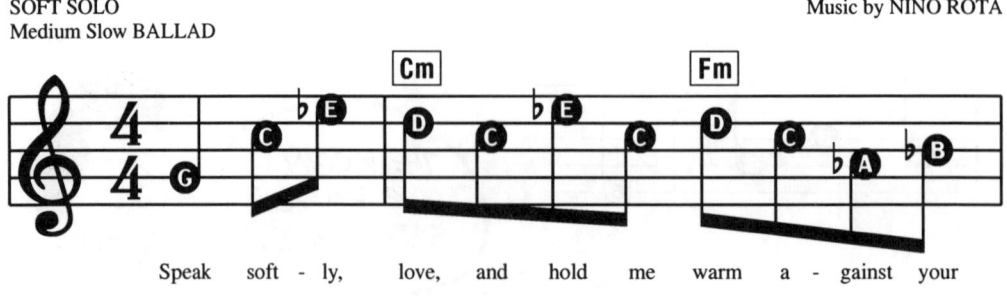

Copyright © 1972 by Famous Music Corporation
International Copyright Secured   All Rights Reserved

26

**VIBES
Optional Substitutes:
MARIMBA, FLUTE, CLARINET**

ALONE

VIBES
SOFT SOLO
Medium ROCK

Words and Music by BILLY STEINBERG
and TOM KELLY

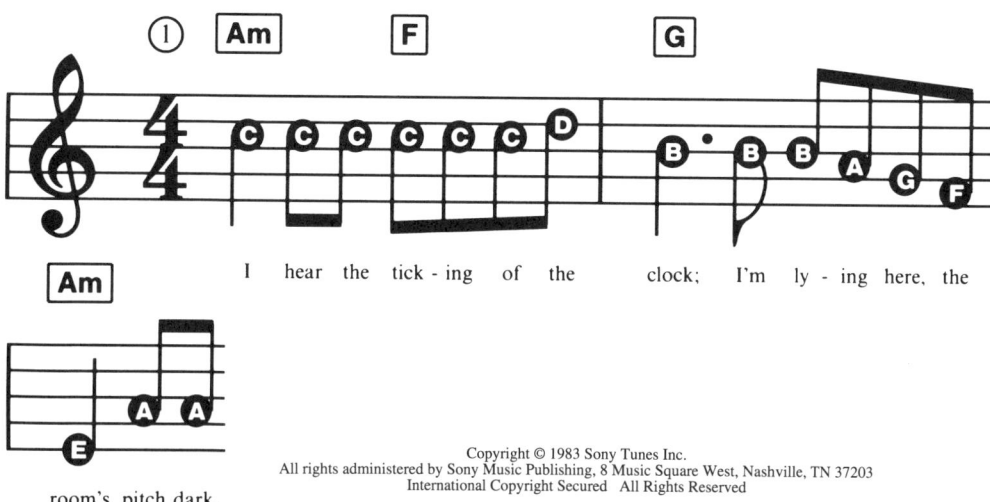

Copyright © 1983 Sony Tunes Inc.
All rights administered by Sony Music Publishing, 8 Music Square West, Nashville, TN 37203
International Copyright Secured   All Rights Reserved

BLUE BAYOU

VIBES
SOFT SOLO
Slow ROCK

Words and Music by ROY ORBISON
and JOE MELSON

Copyright © 1961 (Renewed 1989) ORBI-LEE MUSIC, R-KEY DARKUS MUSIC and ACUFF-ROSE MUSIC, INC.
All rights on behalf of ORBI-LEE MUSIC and R-KEY DARKUS MUSIC administered by WARNER-TAMERLANE PUBLISHING INC.
All Rights Reserved

PIANO/ELECTRIC PIANO
Optional Substitutes:
FLUTE, GUITAR, CLARINET

WHERE EVERYBODY KNOWS YOUR NAME
(Theme From The Paramount Television Series "CHEERS")

PIANO
SOFT SOLO
Medium Fast ROCK

Words and Music by GARY PORTNOY
and JUDY HART ANGELO

Copyright © 1982 by Addax Music Company, Inc.
International Copyright Secured   All Rights Reserved

THE ENTERTAINER

PIANO
BRILLIANT SOLO
Medium SWING

By SCOTT JOPLIN

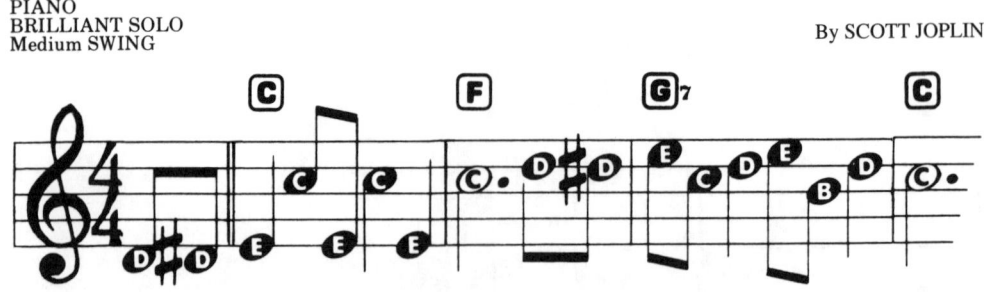

Copyright © 1994 by HAL LEONARD CORPORATION
International Copyright Secured   All Rights Reserved

For a reedy, ragtime sound, try the clarinet voice with this song.

LOVE THEME FROM ST. ELMO'S FIRE

By DAVID FOSTER

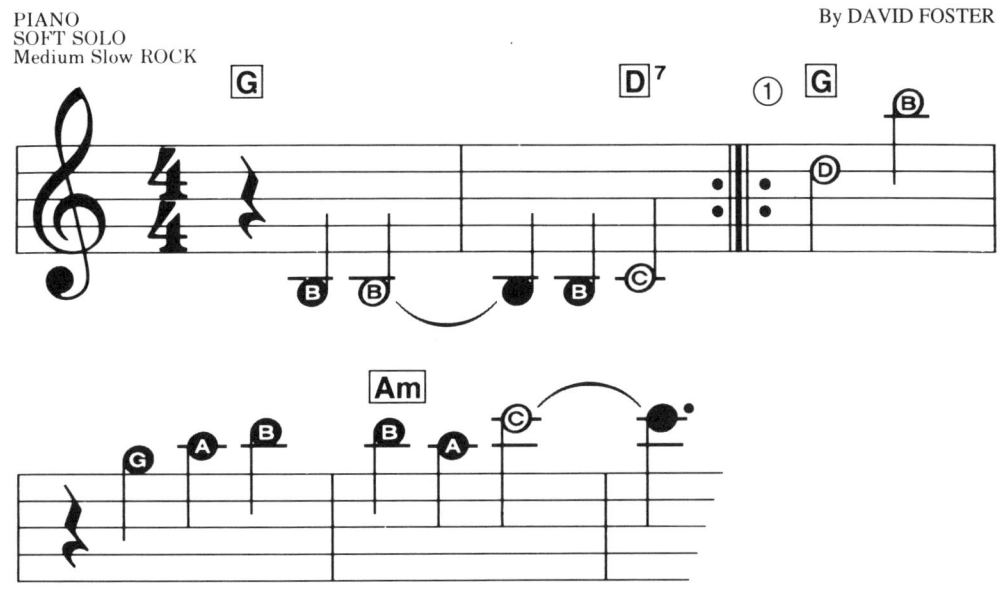

Copyright © 1985 by Gold Horizon Music Corp. and Foster Frees Music, Inc. (BMI)
International Copyright Secured   All Rights Reserved

THEME FROM "TERMS OF ENDEARMENT"

By MICHAEL GORE

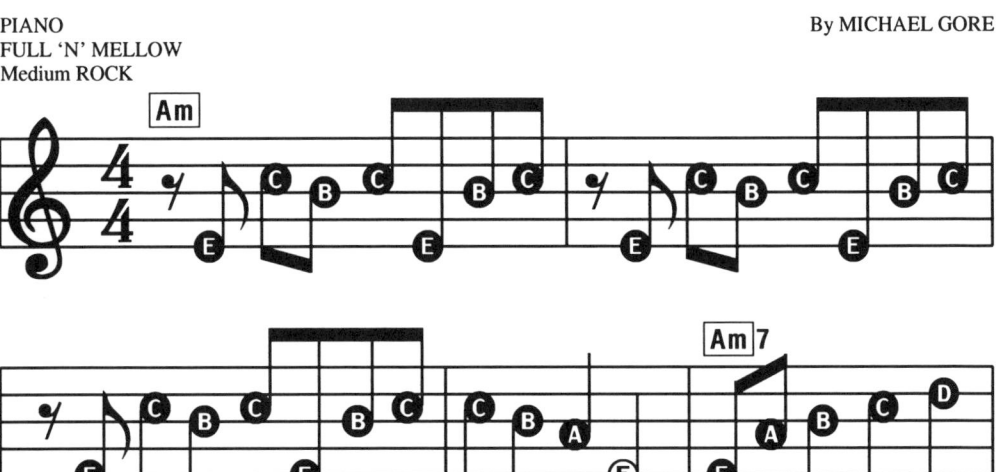

Copyright © 1983 by Ensign Music Corporation
International Copyright Secured   All Rights Reserved

HARPSICHORD
Optional Substitutes:
PIANO, GUITAR

MINUET

HARPSICHORD
SOFT SOLO
Medium WALTZ

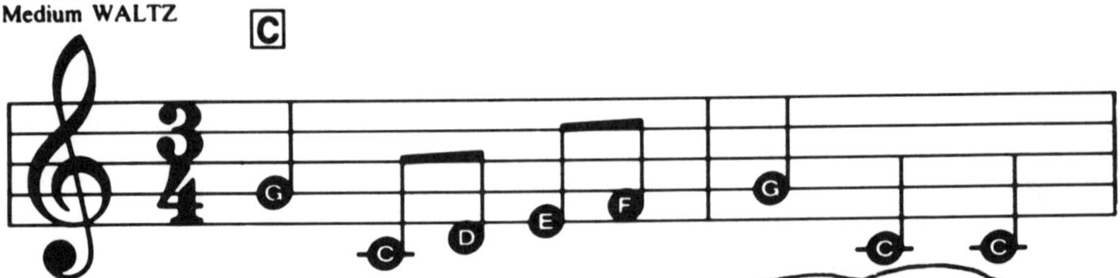

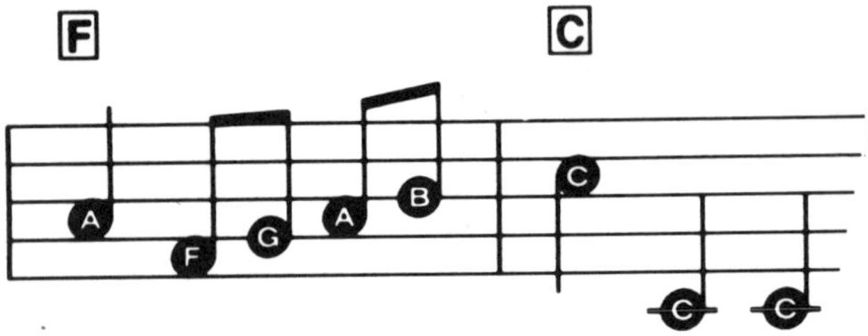

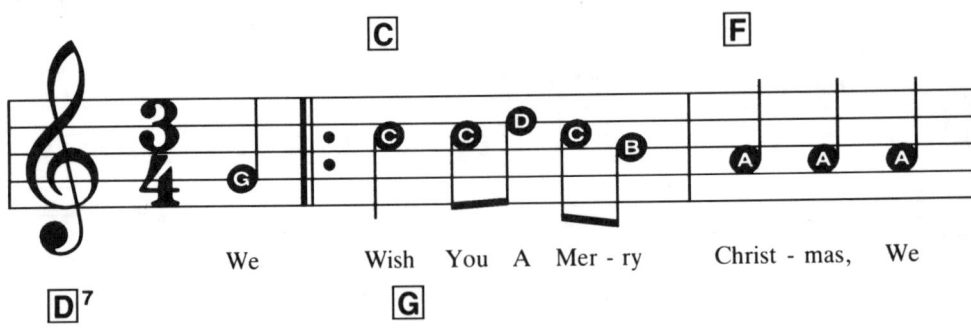

Copyright © 1994 by HAL LEONARD CORPORATION
International Copyright Secured   All Rights Reserved

WE WISH YOU A MERRY CHRISTMAS

HARPSICHORD
FULL 'N' MELLOW
Medium Fast WALTZ

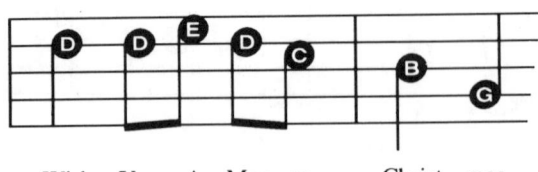

Copyright © 1994 by HAL LEONARD CORPORATION
International Copyright Secured   All Rights Reserved

ACCORDION
Optional Substitutes:
CLARINET, ORGAN, HORN

THAT'S AMORE
(THAT'S LOVE)

Words by JACK BROOKS
Music by HARRY WARREN

ACCORDION
BRILLIANT SOLO
Med. Fast SWING

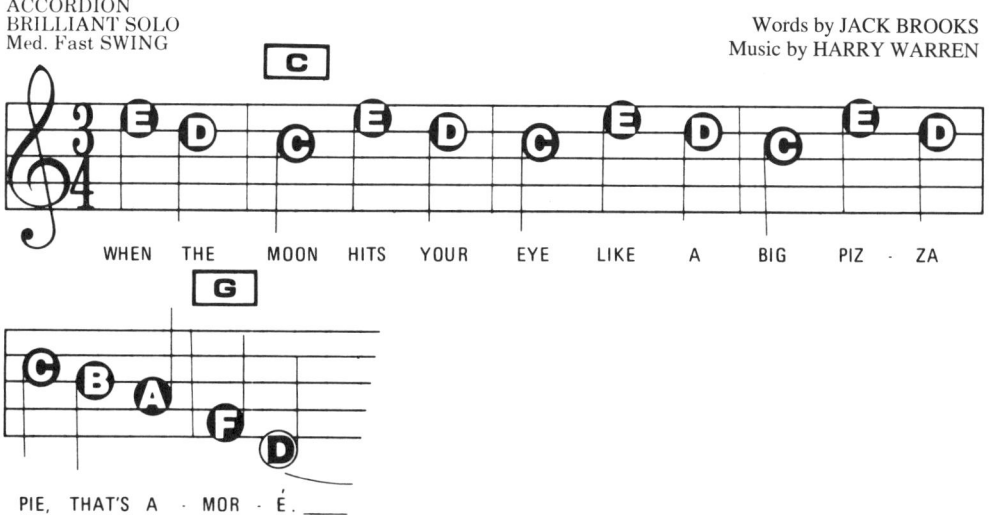

Copyright © 1953 (Renewed 1981) by Paramount Music Corporation and Four Jays Music
International Copyright Secured   All Rights Reserved

BEER BARREL POLKA
(ROLL OUT THE BARREL)

By LEW BROWN, WLADIMIR A. TIMM,
JAROMIR VEJVODA and VASEK ZEMAN

ACCORDION
BRIGHT 'N' BRASSY
Medium Fast POLKA

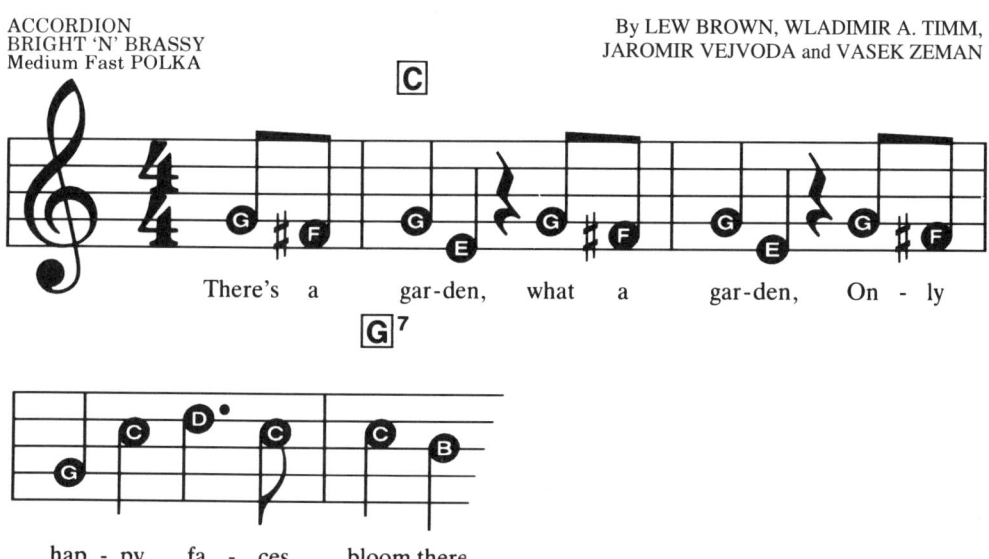

Copyright © 1934 Shapiro, Bernstein & Co., Inc., New York
Copyright Renewed
Copyright © 1939 Shapiro, Bernstein & Co., Inc., New York
Copyright Renewed
International Copyright Secured   All Rights Reserved

GUITAR
Optional Substitutes:
PIANO, SAXOPHONE, CLARINET

THE GAMBLER

GUITAR
BRILLIANT SOLO
Medium SWING

Words and Music by
DON SCHLITZ

1. On a warm sum - mer's eve - nin', On a

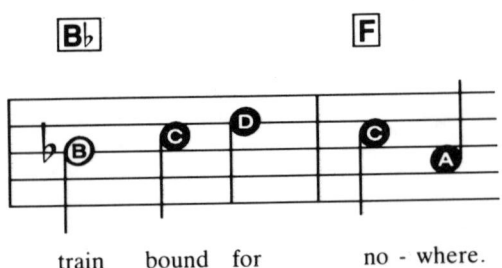

train bound for no - where.

ELECTRIC GUITAR

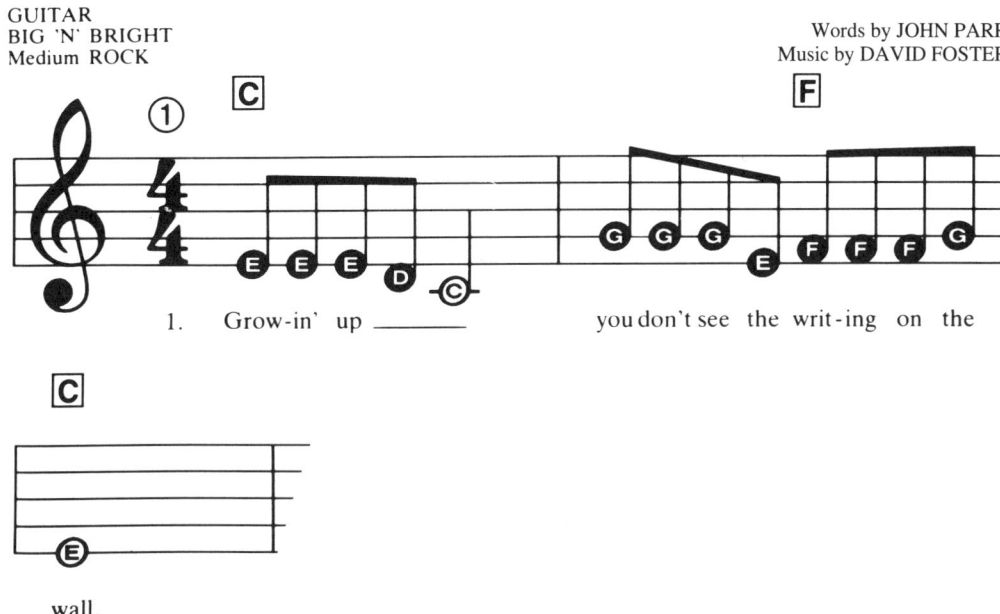

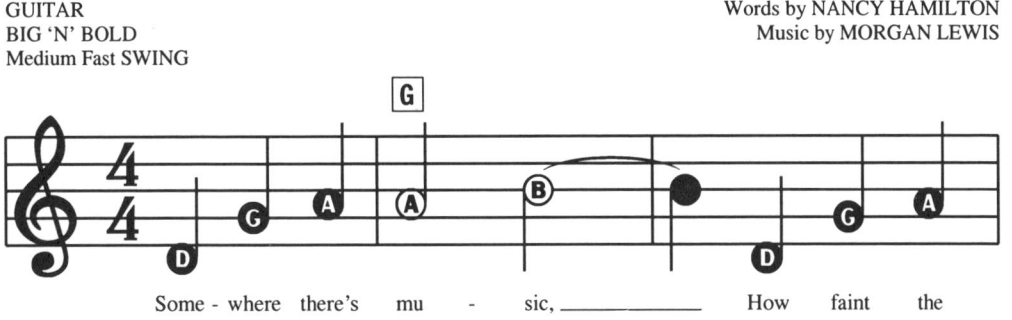

33

STEEL GUITAR/HAWAIIAN GUITAR
Optional Substitutes:
GUITAR, MANDOLIN, PIANO

HAPPY TRAILS

STEEL GUITAR
BRILLIANT SOLO
Slow SWING

Words and Music by
DALE EVANS

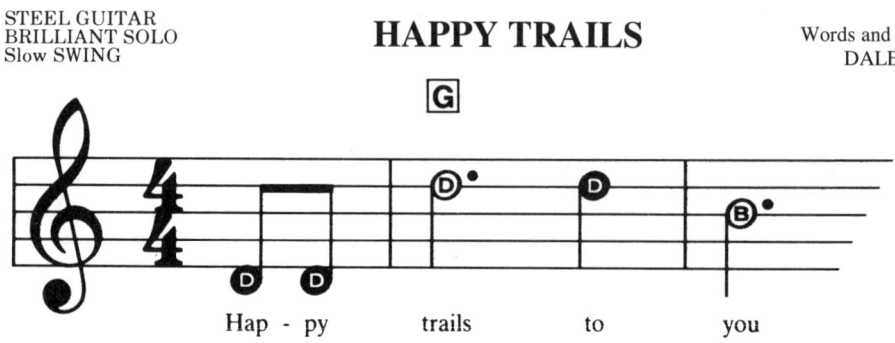

Hap - py   trails   to   you

Copyright © 1951, 1952 (Renewed 1979, 1980) by Paramount-Roy Rogers Music Company, Inc.
International Copyright Secured   All Rights Reserved

BLUE HAWAII
(Theme From The Paramount Picture "BLUE HAWAII")

HAWAIIAN GUITAR
BRILLIANT SOLO
SLOW SWING

Words and Music by LEO RUBIN
and RALPH RAINGER

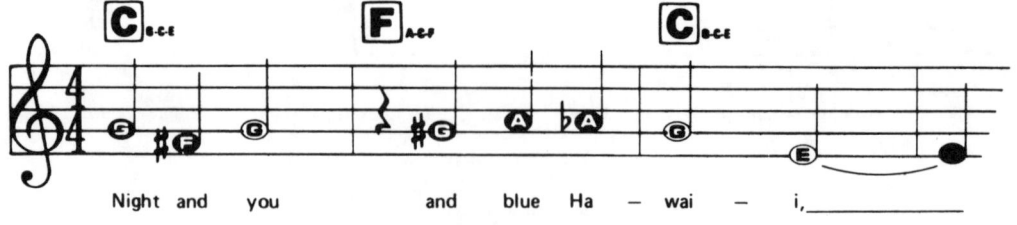

Night and   you   and   blue Ha - wai - i,_____

Copyright © 1936, 1937 (Renewed 1963, 1964) by Famous Music Corporation
International Copyright Secured   All Rights Reserved

CLASSICAL GUITAR
Optional Substitues:
GUITAR, PIANO, HARSICHORD

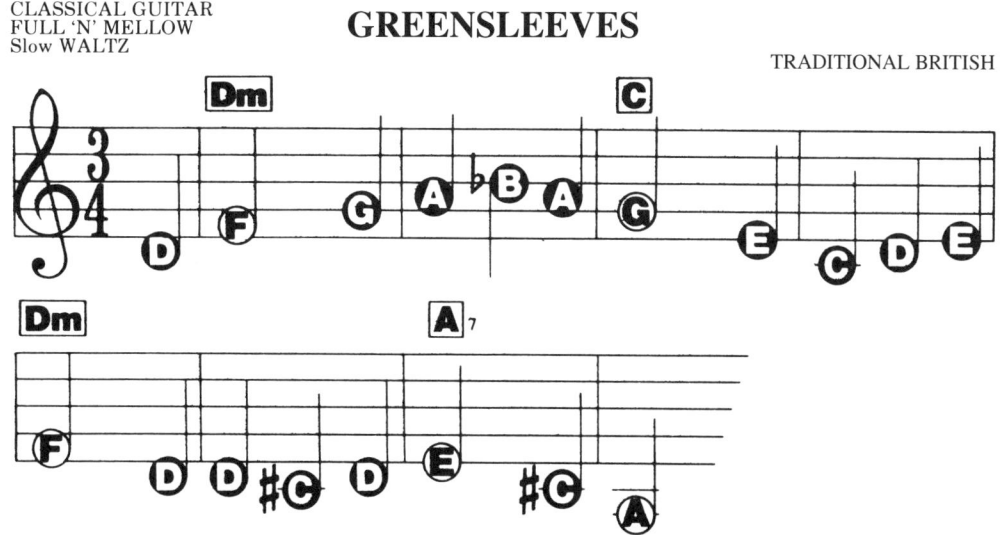

35

BANJO
Optional Substitutes:
GUITAR, PIANO

HEY, MR. BANJO

BANJO
BIG 'N' BOLD
Medium MARCH

By FREDDY MORGAN
and NORMAN MALKIN

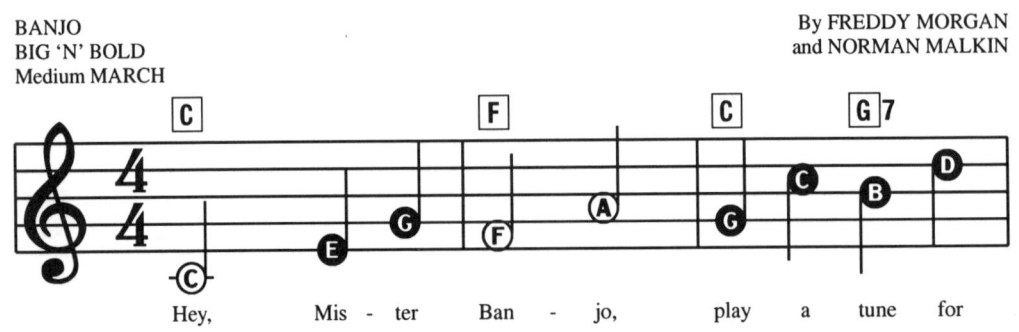

Copyright © 1955 (Renewed) by Mills Music, Inc.
International Copyright Secured   All Rights Reserved

OH SUSANNA

BANJO
BRILLIANT SOLO
Medium SWING

By STEPHEN FOSTER

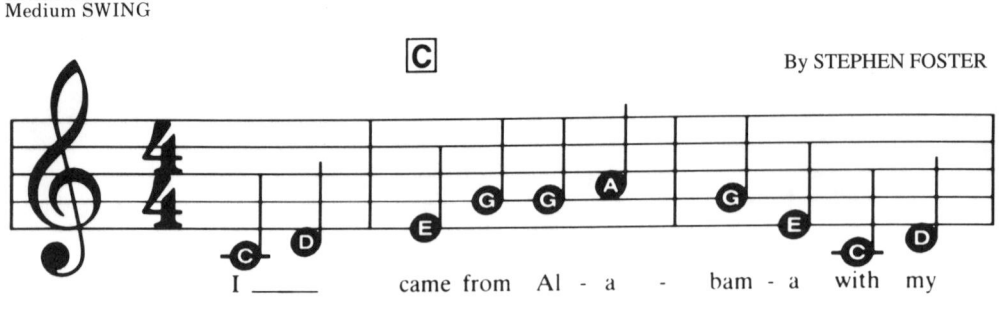

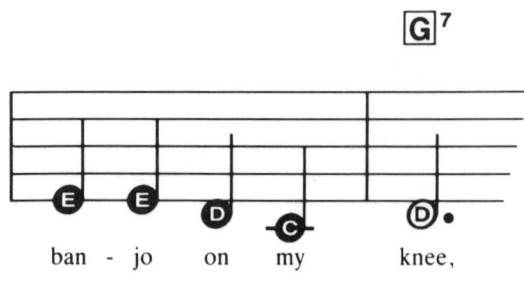

Copyright © 1994 by HAL LEONARD CORPORATION
International Copyright Secured   All Rights Reserved

MANDOLIN
Optional Substitutes:
GUITAR, VIOLIN, ACCORDION, ORGAN

O SOLE MIO

MANDOLIN
SOFT SOLO
Medium BEGUINE

Words by GIOVANNI CAPURRO
Music by EDOARDO DI CAPUA

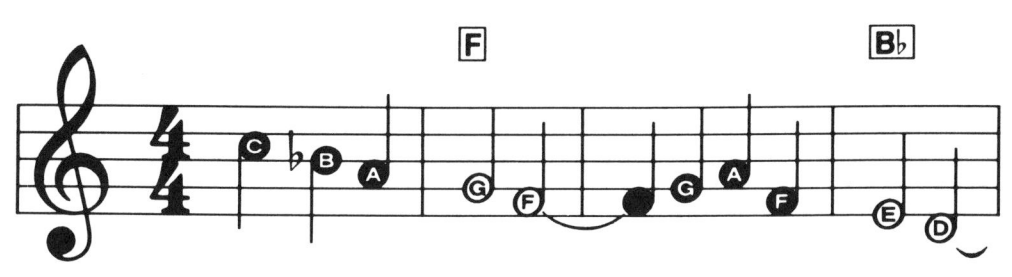

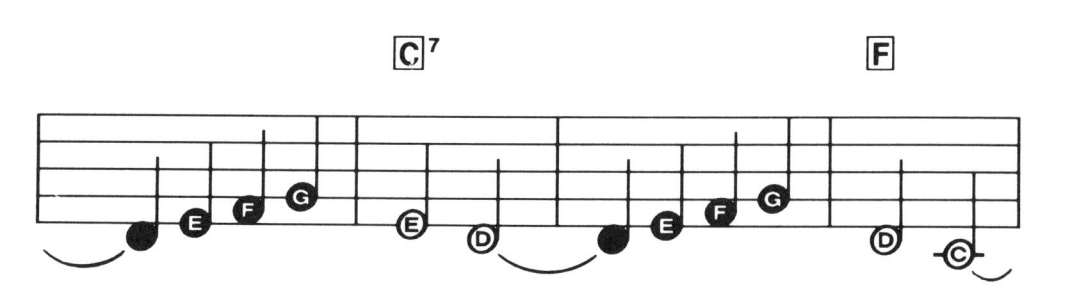

Copyright © 1994 by HAL LEONARD CORPORATION
International Copyright Secured   All Rights Reserved

ORGAN
CHURCH ORGAN/PIPE ORGAN
Optional Substitutes:
STRINGS/VIOLIN, CLARINET, HORN, BRASS, BRASS ENSEMBLE

JOY TO THE WORLD

ORGAN
CLASSICAL
Medium Fast SWING

By ISAAC WATTS

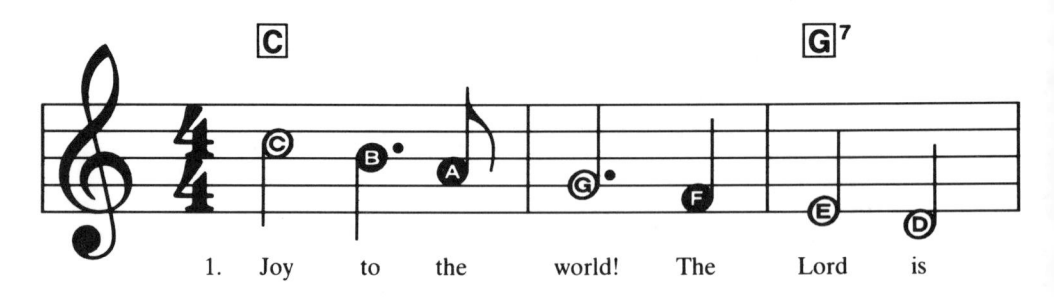

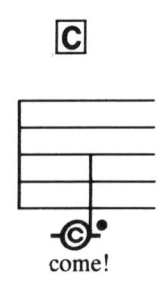

1. Joy to the world! The Lord is come!

Copyright © 1994 by HAL LEONARD CORPORATION
International Copyright Secured   All Rights Reserved

HOLY, HOLY, HOLY

ORGAN
FULL 'N' MELLOW
No Rhythm

Words by REGINALD HEBER
Music by JOHN B. DYKES

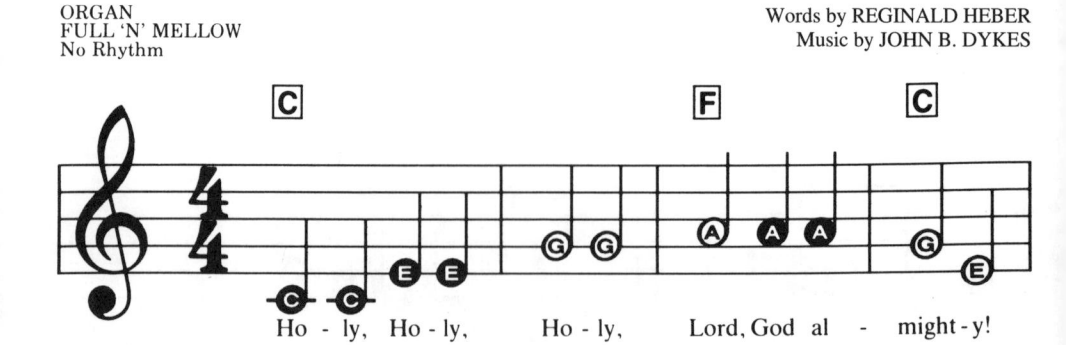

Ho - ly, Ho - ly, Ho - ly, Lord, God al - might - y!

Copyright © 1994 by HAL LEONARD CORPORATION
International Copyright Secured   All Rights Reserved

CALIFORNIA GIRLS

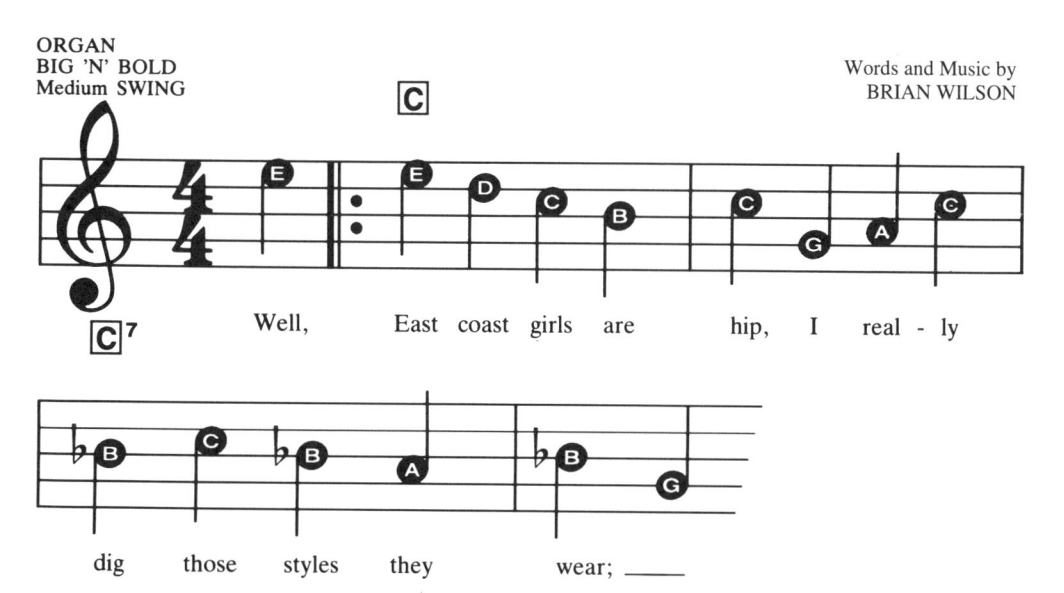

ORGAN
BIG 'N' BOLD
Medium SWING

Words and Music by
BRIAN WILSON

Well, East coast girls are hip, I real - ly dig those styles they wear; ____

Copyright © 1965, 1970 Irving Music, Inc. (BMI)
International Copyright Secured   All Rights Reserved

> EXPERIMENT WITH THE DIFFERENT ORGAN VOICES. EACH ONE HAS A DISTINCT MOOD.

TAKE ME OUT TO THE BALL GAME

ORGAN
FULL 'N' BRILLIANT
Medium WALTZ

Words by JACK NORWORTH
Music by ALBERT VON TILZER

Take! Me out to the ball - game,

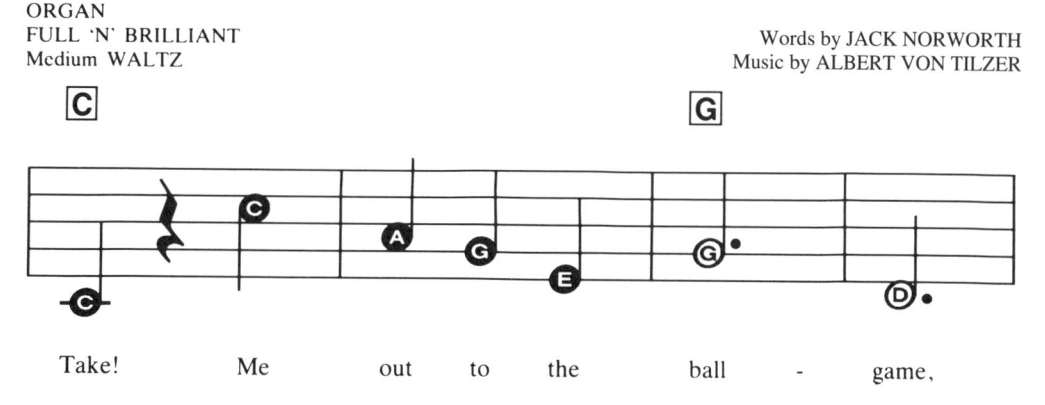

Copyright © 1994 by HAL LEONARD CORPORATION
International Copyright Secured All Rights Reserved

HUMAN NATURE

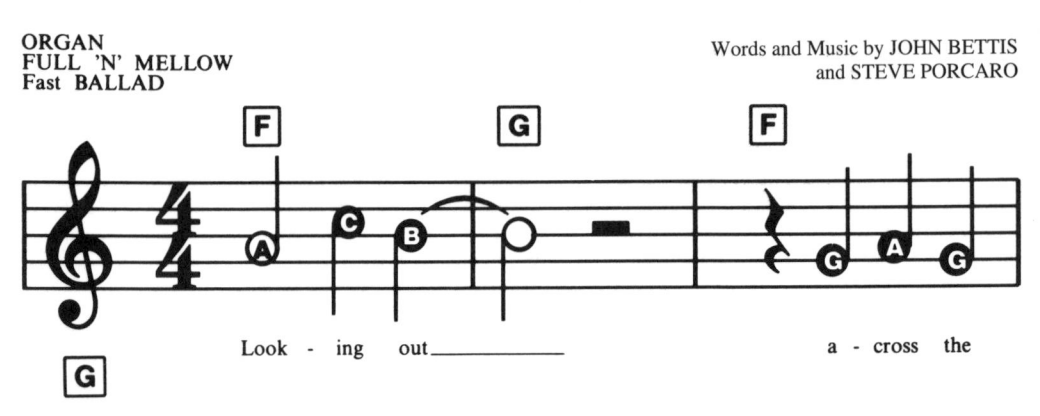

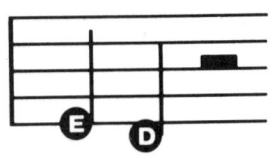

ORGAN
FULL 'N' MELLOW
Fast BALLAD

Words and Music by JOHN BETTIS
and STEVE PORCARO

Look - ing out____ a - cross the night - time,

© 1982 JOHN BETTIS MUSIC and ATV MUSIC CORP.
All rights on behalf of JOHN BETTIS MUSIC administered by WB MUSIC CORP.
All Rights for ATV MUSIC CORP. Controlled and Administered by
EMI BLACKWOOD MUSIC INC. under license from ATV MUSIC CORP.
All Rights Reserved   International Copyright Secured   Used By Permission

TRUE BLUE

ORGAN
SOFT SOLO
Medium SWING

Words and Music by STEPHEN BRAY
and MADONNA CICCONE

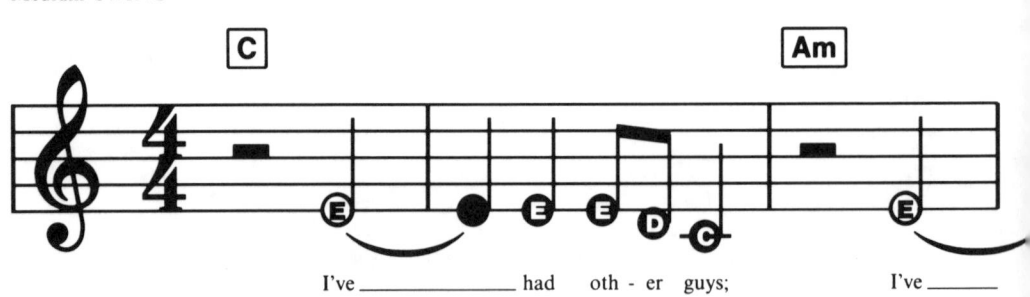

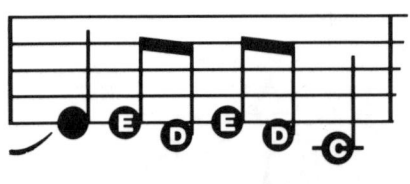

I've____ had oth - er guys; I've____ looked in - to their eyes.

Copyright © 1986 PolyGram International Publishing, Inc., WB Music Corp., Bleu Disque Music Co., Inc. and Webo Girl Publishing, Inc.
International Copyright Secured   All Rights Reserved

CELESTE/CHIMES
Optional Substitutes:
PIANO, FLUTE

BRAHMS' LULLABY

CELESTE
SOFT SOLO
Slow WALTZ

By JOHANNES BRAHMS

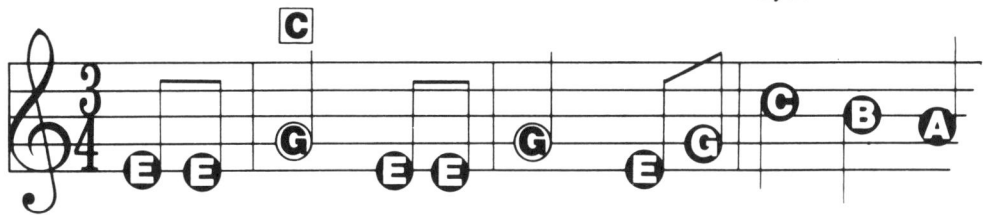

CAROL OF THE BELLS

CHIMES
BRILLIANT SOLO
Medium WALTZ

By M. LEONTOVICH

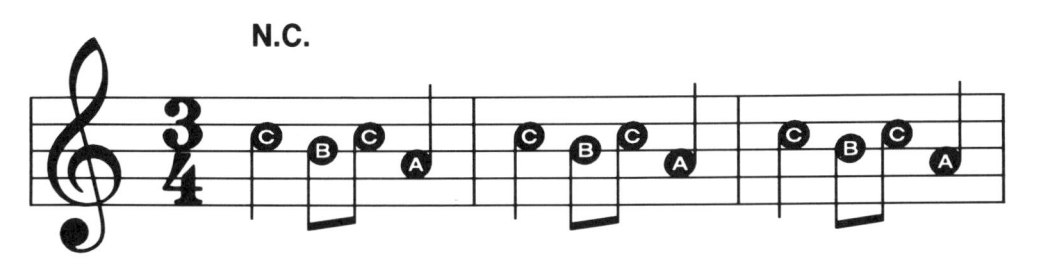

Hark to the bells, Hark to the bells, Tell-ing us all

HORN/FRENCH HORN
Optional Substitutes:
TRUMPET, TROMBONE, CLARINET

RAIDERS MARCH
(From The Paramount Motion Pictures "RAIDERS OF THE LOST ARK,"
"INDIANA JONES AND THE TEMPLE OF DOOM" and
"INDIANA JONES AND THE LAST CRUSADE")

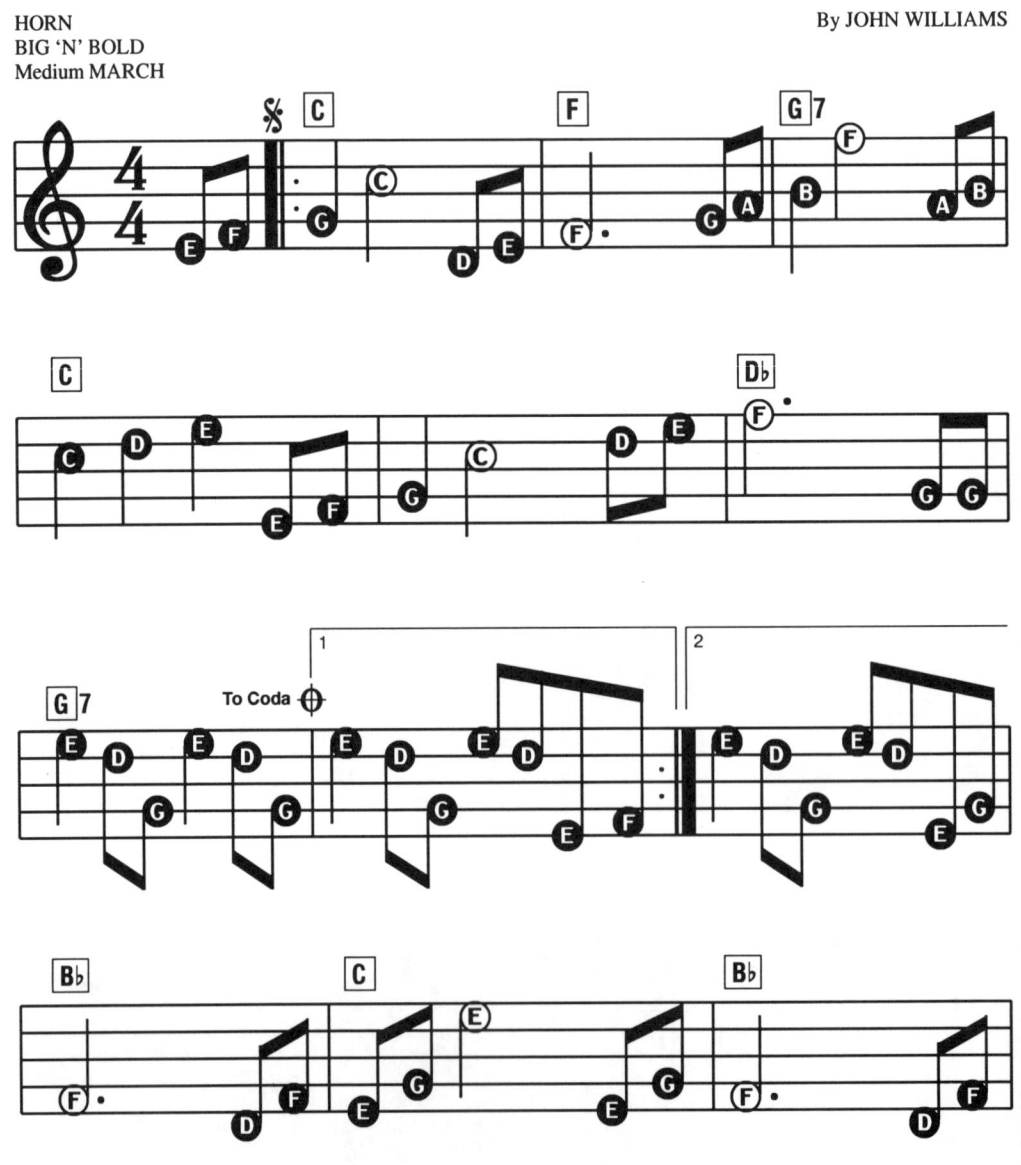

HORN
BIG 'N' BOLD
Medium MARCH

By JOHN WILLIAMS

Copyright © 1981 by Bantha Music and Ensign Music Corporation
This arrangement Copyright © 1994 by Bantha Music and Ensign Music Corporation
All Rights for the World Controlled and Administered by Ensign Music Corporation
International Copyright Secured   All Rights Reserved

LEATHER AND LACE

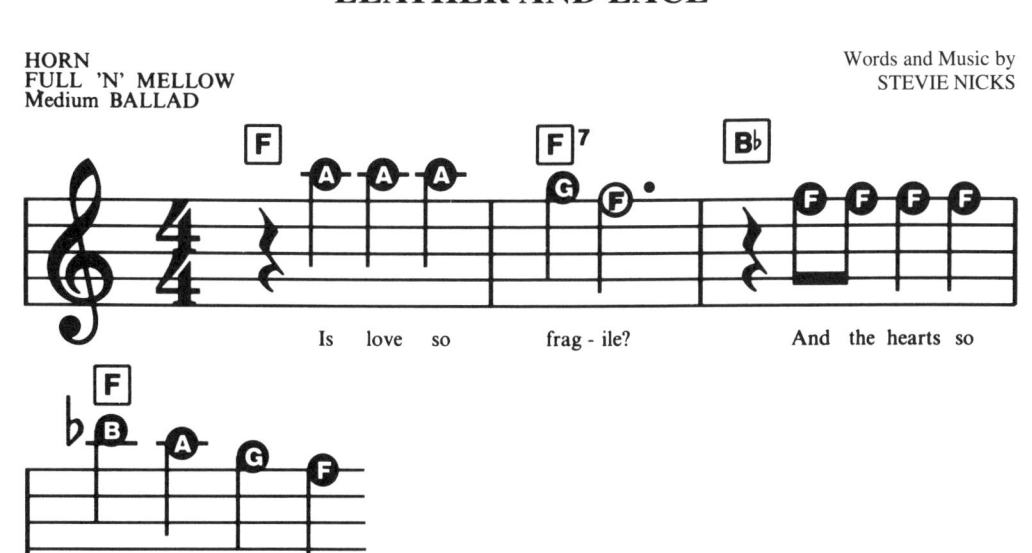

HORN
FULL 'N' MELLOW
Medium BALLAD

Words and Music by
STEVIE NICKS

Is love so frag - ile? And the hearts so hol - low

Copyright © 1981 Welsh Witch Music
All Rights Administered by Sony Music Publishing, 8 Music Square West, Nashville, TN 37203
International Copyright Secured   All Rights Reserved

IF I WERE KING OF THE FOREST

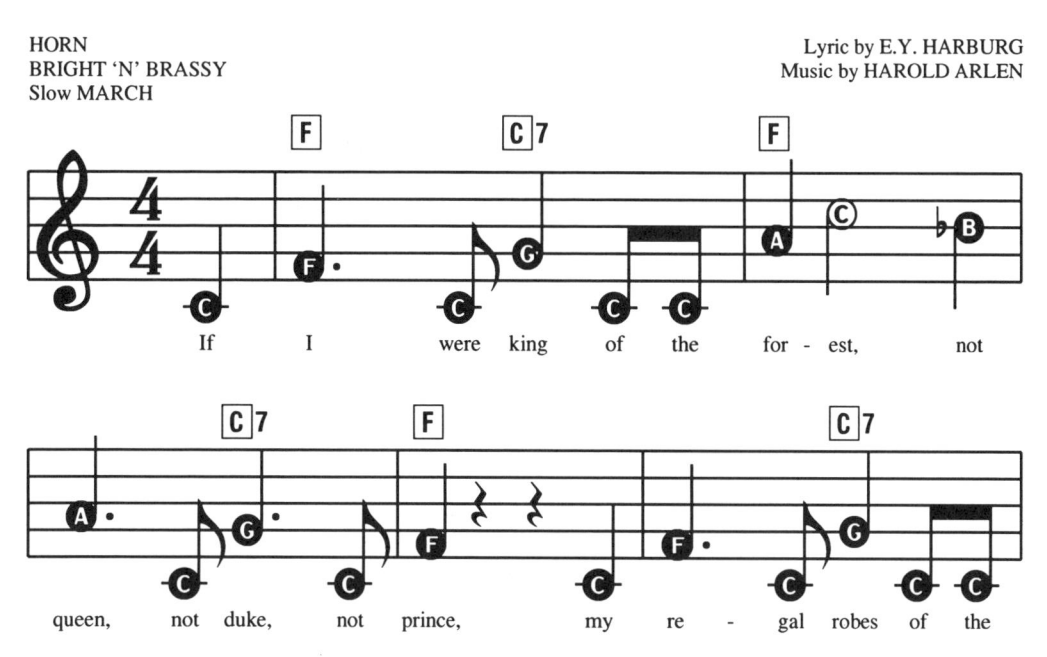

HORN
BRIGHT 'N' BRASSY
Slow MARCH

Lyric by E.Y. HARBURG
Music by HAROLD ARLEN

If I were king of the for - est, not queen, not duke, not prince, my re - gal robes of the

Copyright © 1938, 1939 (Renewed 1960, 1967) METRO-GOLDWYN-MAYER
All Rights excluding Print Controlled by EMI FEIST CATALOG INC.
Worldwide Print Rights Controlled and Administered by CPP/Belwin, Inc., Miami, FL 33014
International Copyright Secured   All Rights Reserved

SYNTHESIZED VOICES

The voice possibilities here are many and varied; therefore, it's difficult to categorize these sounds much beyond dividing them into two groups - those that sound similar to "real" instruments and those that don't.

A good example is any voice whose name includes the word *brass,* e.g. Wah Brass, Synthe Brass, Funny Brass, etc. On some instruments, the sound might resemble a trumpet; on others, a trombone. On others, however, it could be a totally new sound. This generalization applies to most voice groups related to synthesized sounds.

Try the following song excerpts using any synthesizer-type voices you have. There's a real cross-section here - you should have fun with it.

THEME FROM "STAR TREK"

BRILLIANT SOLO
Medium Fast DISCO

Words by GENE RODDENBERRY
Music by ALEXANDER COURAGE

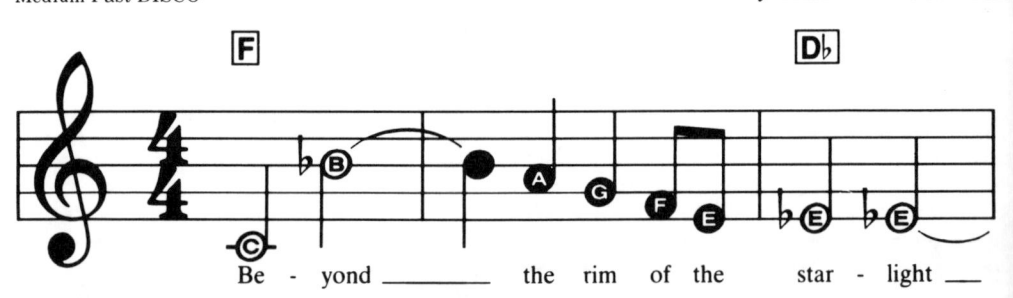

Be - yond ____ the rim of the star - light ____

Copyright © 1966, 1970 by Bruin Music Company
International Copyright Secured   All Rights Reserved

THEME FROM "CLOSE ENCOUNTERS™ OF THE THIRD KIND"

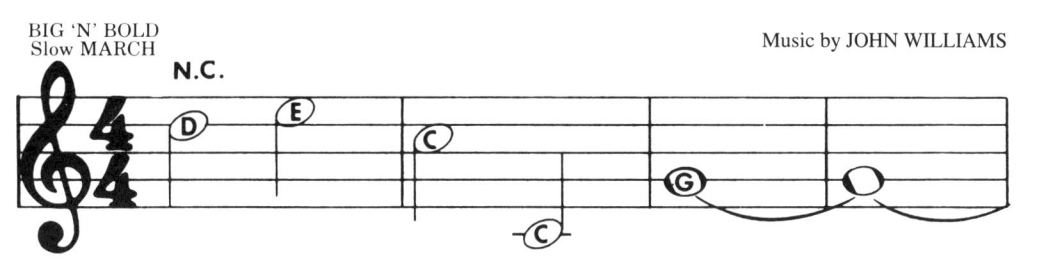

BIG 'N' BOLD
Slow MARCH

Music by JOHN WILLIAMS

Copyright © 1977 by Gold Horizon Music Corp.
This arrangement Copyright © 1979 by Gold Horizon Music Corp.
International Copyright Secured   All Rights Reserved

AXEL F

FULL 'N' MELLOW
Medium DISCO

By HAROLD FALTERMEYER

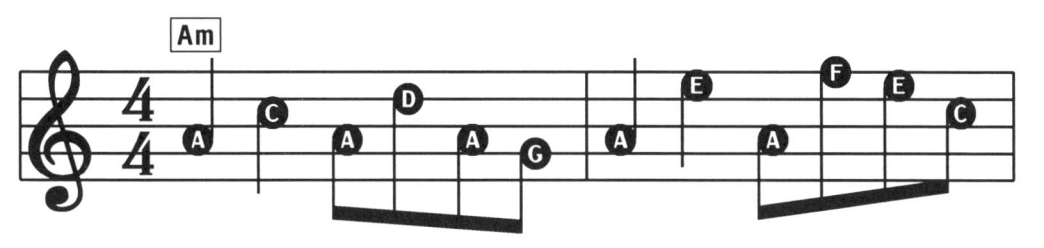

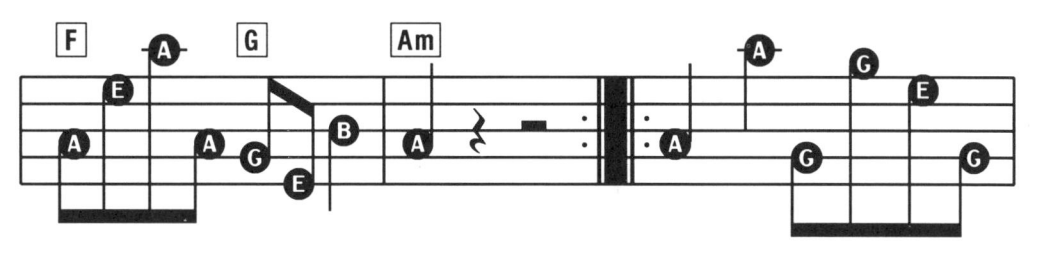

Copyright © 1984, 1985 by Famous Music Corporation
International Copyright Secured   All Rights Reserved

45

The HOW TO's of
EASY ABC MUSIC FOR BEGINNERS

Playing The Melody

Melodies are made up of **notes** and are played by your right hand on the upper keyboard, or solo section. Seven letters — A through G — repeated over and over, name every note you'll ever play. They name every key on your keyboard too. Speed Music makes it easy by using these letters in each note.

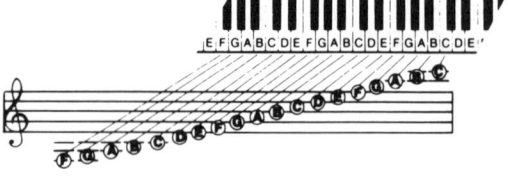

Sharps and Flats

In Easy-Play Speed Music, a **sharp** (♯) tells you to play the very next key to the right and a **flat** (♭) tells you to play the very next key to the left. These are usually black keys.

Time Values

In music, time is measured in **beats**. The illustration shows the types of notes you'll play and how many beats each type gets.

Rests are shown in the lower part of the illustration, along with the number of beats each types gets. A rest indicates a period of silence, when you don't play — they still must be counted, however.

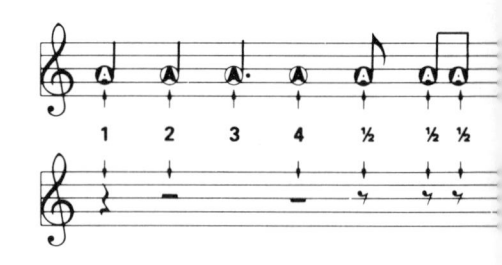

The Staff, Measures and Bar Lines

The **staff** consists of five lines and four spaces and each is named with one of the letters A through G. Any note that appears on one of the lines or in one of the spaces is called by that letter-name.

The S-shaped symbol at the beginning of the staff is called the **treble clef** and tells you all the notes that follow are to be played by your right hand.

The staff is divided into equal sections by using vertical lines called **bar lines**. The sections between the bar lines are called **measures**.

Time Signature

The two numbers at the beginning of a song are known as the **time signature**. The top number indicates the number of beats in each measure. The bottom number 4 tells you each quarter note (♩) receives one beat.

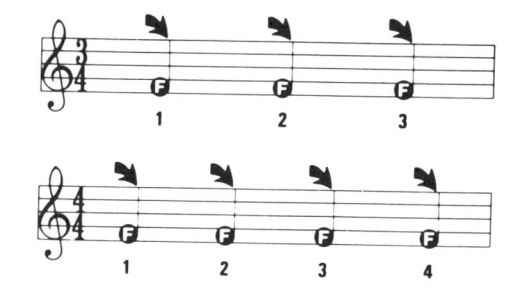

Ties

A **tie** is a curved line connecting notes on the same line or in the same space. It indicates the first note is struck and then held for the total time value of the tied notes.

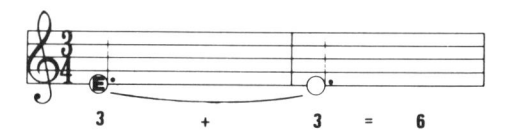

‖:Repeat Signs:‖ and Double Endings

These tell you to play certain parts of a song more than once. If a song has more than one set of lyrics, you'll generally see repeat signs.

Sometimes a repeated song, or part of a song, has two different endings. In these cases, **double endings** are used.

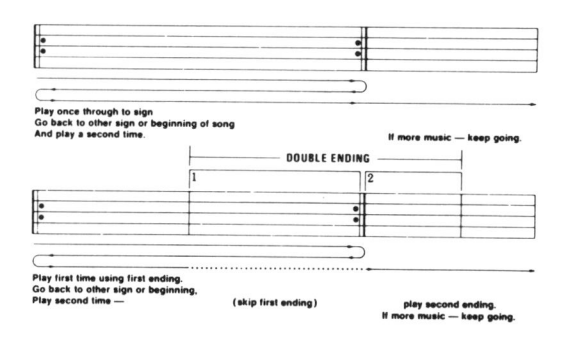

Playing the Accompaniment

Accompaniment consists of **chords**, indicated by **chord symbols** in your music: [C] [G]7

Generally, there are three ways to play chords: One finger, traditional or three-note Easy-Play chords. Your owner's guide can help you decide which methods your keyboard is capable of. Be sure to try them all.

N.C. tells you "No Chord" is played — just the right-hand melody.

Substitute chords appear in brackets [ ] to the right of a chord symbol — use whichever sounds best to you.

Like substitutes, **optional chords** are up to your taste and preference. They're not necessary to the song but they do make the accompaniment more interesting. These are the **small** chord symbols that appear above the melody. The small 7 that appears to the right of certain chords indicates another form of optional chord. A seventh is a fuller-sounding chord. However, they are not necessary — it's a matter of personal taste.

47

SONG EXCERPTS

20	AIN'T MISBEHAVIN'
27	ALONE
45	AXEL F
31	BEER BARREL POLKA (ROLL OUT THE BARREL)
27	BLUE BAYOU
34	BLUE HAWAII
41	BRAHMS' LULLABY
39	CALIFORNIA GIRLS
17	CARAVAN
41	CAROL OF THE BELLS
16	COVENTRY CAROL
25	CRYING
24	CZARDAS
28	THE ENTERTAINER
20	FIVE FOOT TWO, EYES OF BLUE (HAS ANYBODY SEEN MY GIRL?)
32	THE GAMBLER
23	GEORGIA ON MY MIND
17	GOING HOME
35	GREENSLEEVES
34	HAPPY TRAILS
36	HEY, MR. BANJO
38	HOLY, HOLY, HOLY
33	HOW HIGH THE MOON
40	HUMAN NATURE
14	I JUST CALLED TO SAY I LOVE YOU
22	I'M GETTING SENTIMENTAL OVER YOU
43	IF I WERE KING OF THE FOREST
18	IN THE MOOD
21	INTO THE GROOVE
38	JOY TO THE WORLD
18	JUST THE WAY YOU ARE
43	LEATHER AND LACE
29	LOVE THEME FROM ST. ELMO'S FIRE
25	MIDNIGHT COWBOY
30	MINUET
19	THEME FROM NEW YORK, NEW YORK
37	O SOLE MIO
36	OH SUSANNA
42	RAIDERS MARCH
16	RHIANNON
13	SAILING
21	SIR DUKE
7	THE SKATERS
26	SPEAK SOFTLY, LOVE (LOVE THEME FROM THE GODFATHER)
33	ST. ELMO'S FIRE (MAN IN MOTION)
22	STAND BY ME
19	STAR DUST
23	SUDDENLY
44	THEME FROM "STAR TREK"
39	TAKE ME OUT TO THE BALL GAME
12	TAKE MY BREATH AWAY (LOVE THEME FROM TOP GUN)
29	THEME FROM "TERMS OF ENDEARMENT"
31	THAT'S AMORE (THAT'S LOVE)
24	THEME FROM ICE CASTLES (THROUGH THE EYES OF LOVE)
45	THEME FROM "CLOSE ENCOUNTERS™ OF THE THIRD KIND"
15	A TIME FOR US (LOVE THEME FROM ROMEO AND JULIET)
13	TOO FAT POLKA (SHE'S TOO FAT FOR ME)
40	TRUE BLUE
26	TRUE COLORS
30	WE WISH YOU A MERRY CHRISTMAS
15	WHAT'S LOVE GOT TO DO WITH IT
28	WHERE EVERYBODY KNOWS YOUR NAME (THEME FROM "CHEERS")